GW01319776

Prophet for Our Times

Peter Deunov, (Beinsa Douno) who lived in Bulgaria from 1864 to 1944, was a great and inspired teacher of the Perennial Wisdom – the thread of truth running through all the major world religions which links us to the source of all things, the Divine. All those who came into contact with him were profoundly moved by his grace and his deep spirituality. His teachings are essentially a prescription for living in harmony with others, with the earth and with the Divine, and are relevant to all people, whatever their faith or beliefs. Paneurhythmy, the form of sacred dance developed by him, is intended for all those who wish to experience harmony in their lives, for, in the sacred dance, we mirror the macrocosmic order of the heavens. As we dance the circle, we create within ourselves a still centre, and turn our spirit back to its divine source.

David Lorimer, who compiled and edited this book, is a well-known author and lecturer on spiritual matters. He is director of The Scientific and Medical Network and the International Association for Near Death Studies (U.K.). He came into contact with the teachings of Peter Deunov some five years ago and is now actively involved in his work. He is the author of *Survival* (1984) and *Whole in One* (1990).

Also Available

CIRCLE OF SACRED DANCE
Peter Deunov's Paneurhythmy

Prophet for our Times

The Life and Teachings of
Peter Deunov

Edited with an introduction by
David Lorimer

First published by Element Books Ltd 1991
© Vega 2002
Text © David Lorimer 1991

All rights reserved. No part of this book may be
reproduced, stored in a retrieval system or transmitted in
any form or by any means, electronic, mechanical,
photocopying, recording or otherwise, without the prior
permission in writing of the copyright owners

ISBN 1-84333-431-3

A catalogue record for this book is available
from the British Library

Published in 2002 by
Vega
64 Brewery Road
London, N7 9NT

A member of **Chrysalis** Books plc

Visit our website at www.chrysalisbooks.co.uk

Printed in Great Britain
by Lightning Source
Cover designed by Design Revolution, Brighton

Contents

This book is lovingly dedicated to
Krum Vagarov
(1907–1991)
a faithful disciple
of
The Master
Beinsa Duono

Introduction

THE BULGARIAN BACKGROUND

When people discover that I am learning Bulgarian, they are usually surprised, a surprise which turns to astonishment when I inform them that I have a Bulgarian teacher two miles from my home in the Cotswolds! Why Bulgarian? For most people Bulgarian means drinkable cabernet sauvignon at affordable prices or, possibly, rose essence which is used by perfume manufacturers as a raw material. Many will have heard of the Balkan Mountains and the Black Sea, but that will probably be the sum total of their geographical knowledge of the area. They will almost certainly not have heard of the Spiritual Master Beinsa Douno (Peter Deunov), the author of the selections in this book, and the reason why I am in the process of learning Bulgarian.

My acquaintance with Beinsa Douno and the Brotherhood of Light goes back to 1985 when I first read some books by Omraam Mikhael Aivanhov on the way to an Easter holiday in Crete. I discovered that Aivanhov had spent twenty years as a pupil with Beinsa Douno before coming to France in 1937 where he taught until his death in 1986. It then turned out that there were a few people in London and Paris who knew more about the original work in Bulgaria, especially Anna Bertoli who edited a quarterly review, *Le Grain de Blé*, for thirty-two years until the summer of 1989. She and some other Bulgarians in Paris had known Beinsa Douno personally, thus establishing a living connection. I also found out that Gerard Nizet, with his publishing house, Le Courrier du Livre, had been editing volumes of Douno's teaching since the early 1950s. It was fortunate that I was earning my living by teaching French, so the reading of hundreds of pages in that language presented no difficulties. Very little has actually been published in English, and what there is has long since been out of print. This introductory selection, therefore, is the first book to appear in English for more than twenty years.

In August 1989 I finally went to Bulgaria, arriving in Sofia very late at night to a warm welcome from some Bulgarian friends who piled our luggage into their cars. The hotel was not easy to find and I had doubts about the ability of the hesitant engine of my friend's Trabant to keep going at all. My opinion of the car's stamina had risen immensely by the end of my stay when it had negotiated mountain tracks and slopes that might have defeated many more elegant western models.

We went up to the Moussala camp the following day, via a ski lift taking us to 7500 feet. The weather on the first evening was unpromising as fog and low cloud completely obscured the view and barely enabled us to make out the lake some 600 feet below. By the following morning, however, the cloud was lifting and we were able to climb the 1000 feet to the ridge from where the sunrise can be seen towards the Balkans. Camping readers will be familiar with the joys and discomforts of the outdoor life which are amplified by rugged conditions in the mountains. Mornings can be bitterly cold but the midday sun is scorching, and the rain, when it comes, is often relentless. The changing weather is a symbol of the changing external circumstances in our lives.

The sunrise was the most mystical moment of the day. In the distance, the hazy shades of other mountain ranges kept silent vigil as the red orb edged up out of the mist and slowly gained in splendour and radiance. We sang some of the Master's songs and recited prayers and formulas. Nature was our temple, the majestic backdrop of the high peaks our open-air cathedral. Before breakfast we performed the six and twenty-two gymnastic exercises, dancing the paneurhythmy later on when the violonist's fingers had defrosted.

One of the most spectacular sites for dancing the paneur-hythmy is a grassy space overlooking the Maritsa Lakes. The air is crystal clear, the colours are sharp and the scene sublimely beautiful. One day we made an excursion to the Maritsa Lakes, taking our picnic with us and climbing up towards Moussala in the afternoon. Above the lakes is the source of the River Maritsa, surrounded by a natural amphitheatre of jagged ridges; it is supposed to be one of the sites visited by Orpheus. By the time we climbed right up to Moussala, the highest peak in the range, the weather had turned cold and cloudy, and we were glad of a cup of tea to warm us up. We returned to base at around nine in the evening.

After over a week in Moussala it was time to move to the other camp. Horses were sent for in order to take the kit down, the 'kitchen' was dismantled and pots hidden in the rocks for next year. We made the journey via one of the famous hot springs and arrived at Sikiritsa Place in early evening. This camp, situated in the pine trees, is much larger; its lower altitude makes it less rigorous and there are many musicians in the camp who are happy to give concerts round the fire at night. We had one in the rain and another by moonlight. Wild flowers abounded in the open spaces undisturbed by human hand. Further up, the Seven Lakes beckoned, but the weather was too unstable to make the excursion for three days.

The morning of our Seven Lakes journey was a spell in paradise. We wended our way up to the camp by the second lake where we stopped for breakfast and visited the Mount of Prayer, the place from where one sees the sunrise and where the Master Beinsa Douno gave his 5 am talks during summer camp. The site is sacred, guarded by a stone on which a formula is inscribed. The Lake of Contemplation looks like a deep blue pearl. We stopped occasionally to rest, meditate and pray, finally coming down to the second lake where the first camp had taken place in 1929. In 1939 there had been more than 500 people.

Coming back to Sofia from the mountains is rather a jolt, especially when so much of it consists of faceless apartment blocks. Discussions with my friends revealed no hope of a change of regime and, yet, four months later, I heard the news of the fall of the government while driving from a conference in Cornwall. It seemed quite incredible.

The atmosphere in 1990 was naturally much more open. It had been possible to hold the first public meeting since 1944 and whole-page features on Beinsa Douno and his teaching were appearing in popular newspapers. Political freedom, though, is no guarantee of economic efficiency: the shops were empty, petrol was scarce. There is a great deal of spadework to be done before Bulgaria achieves a measure of real stability, but the people are ever-hopeful and good-humoured. An old sister told me in 1989 that Beinsa Douno had predicted that conditions for his work would be extremely difficult for forty-five years after his death in 1944. But the source is beginning to flow again and the dormant grain of wheat will be able to germinate.

THE SPIRITUAL DEVELOPMENT OF BULGARIA

The coming of Beinsa Douno to Bulgaria marks the third major spiritual impulse in its history. The first two came through Orpheus and the Bogomils. All three are historical manifestations of the White Brotherhood, the great community of the divine world, of those beings who serve God. It is the Brotherhood or Fellowship of Divine Love, Divine Wisdom and Divine Truth and is responsible for all the new spiritual impulses given to the Earth. The school of the White Brotherhood, Beinsa Douno explains, is the luminous path of Love, Wisdom and Truth; the fundamental objective of the school, however, is Love: Wisdom and Truth play a supporting role. This great community is in direct contact with God, and with Christ, the manifestation of God.

The Bogomils

In a lecture answering a number of queries about the Bogomils and their relationship to other spiritual movements, Beinsa Douno explained that there were three branches of the Bogomil school.

Hermeticism.   The first branch was the Hermeticism of Egypt which migrated to Thrace via Persia and reappeared with Orpheus, thought to have lived in the Rhodope Mountains, the neighbouring range to Rila. Orpheus, in turn, was the source from which flowed the Pythagorean and Platonic schools; both these schools taught a doctrine of transmigration and purification of the soul. The impulse reappeared in the Florentine Renaissance with Pico dela Mirandola and flourished in Cambridge during the seventeenth century. Dean Inge of St Paul's was perhaps the last great Christian Neo-Platonist in our own time with his remarkable Gifford Lectures on the philosophy of Plotinus.

The Essenes. The second branch operated in Palestine under the aegis of the Essenes. Since the Nag Hammadi discoveries in the mid-1940s, the Essenes have become much better known and scholarship has revealed hitherto unknown aspects of their doctrines. There has also been a series of books by Dr Edmond Bordeaux Szekely, founder of the International Biogenic Society, who thought of the Essenes as an early ecological community. His writings are often inspired but I know of no one who can cross-check his sources. Contemporary writers do, however, bear out the picture of a dedicated community of people who integrated a healthy lifestyle with systematic spiritual practice and an emphasis on purity.

The Bogomils. The third branch arose in Bulgaria in the course of the tenth century and were called the Bogomils, literally meaning 'beloved of God'. Before expanding on their views, lifestyle and influence, it is worth tracing the events which gave rise to the movement.

The key figure is the Khan Boris, who succeeded to the throne in AD852. In order to unify the disparate elements of his country, he realized that it would be politic to embrace Christianity – but which version, East or West? At first, in 862, he concluded an alliance with Louis the German, an arrangement which lasted only two years before Bulgaria was invaded by the Byzantine Emperor Michael and Boris was forced to capitulate. He then accepted baptism in the name of his people, setting the scene for the eventual development of a Slavonic form of Christianity. The pagan masses, however, resented the Church's attempts to destroy their ancient traditions and beliefs and were consequently receptive to the teaching of the wandering Paulician heretics.

Then, in 866, Boris wavered to the West again, sending envoys to Rome with a request for instruction in 'the pure

Christian faith', his underlying aim being to secure a greater degree of autonomy for his church than the Byzantines were prepared to allow. A further reversal took place in 869 when a council decided to attach Bulgaria once again to the eastern Church and expel the western missionaries as impostors. Doctrinal struggles doubtless contributed to the growth of heresy by undermining the prestige of both sides and producing a climate of religious instability. This was exacerbated by widespread economic disruptions and social inequalities, factors which provided a focus for resistance against the authorities.

The pioneering figure of Saint John of Rila embodied a search for sanctity which was allied to an almost outright condemnation of the world as an obstacle to salvation, a feeling which resonated strongly with heretics such as the Paulicians who simply equated matter with evil and strove to overcome its fetters. The monastic ideal, however, went into sharp decline, so much so that the priest Cosmas, writing soon after 972, directed his attacks as much to the prevalent abuses of monasticism as to the heresy of the Bogomils.

As is so often the case in ecclesiastical history, we owe the account of Bogomil doctrines to one of its principal opponents. Cosmas begins his treatise thus:

> It came to pass that in the land of Bulgaria, in the days of the Orthodox Tsar Peter, there appeared a priest by the name of Bogomil, but in truth 'not beloved of God'. He was the first who began to preach in Bulgaria a heresy, of whose vagaries we shall speak below.[1]

The Bogomils' pursuit of moral purity was clearly an embarrassment to their Orthodox opponents who saw it as a heinous form of hypocrisy, all the more so given the generally dissolute reputation of the priesthood. Thus Cosmas writes:

> The heretics in appearance are lamb-like, gentle, modest and silent, and pale from hypocritical fasting. They do not talk idly, nor laugh loudly, nor show any curiosity . . . outwardly they do everything so as not to be distinguished from righteous Christians, but inwardly they are ravening wolves . . .[2]

He goes on to say that people are struck by their humility and ask them how to save their souls. This then gives the heretics the opportunity to 'sow the tares of their teaching, blaspheming the traditions and rules of the Holy Church'. He also comments on their tenacity, saying that 'you will more easily bring a beast to reason than a heretic; for just as a swine passes by a pearl and collects dirt, so do the heretics swallow their own filth'. Graphic language indeed.

Obolensky (see Notes, p. 38) rightly finds it significant that the Orthodox repudiation was mainly concerned with the moral and social aspects of the heresy, rather than with doctrinal considerations. These are, nevertheless, important and share many features with other dualist heresies whose ancestry can be traced back to early gnosticism. While the Paulicians embraced a thoroughgoing metaphysical dualism with good and evil principles of equal status, the Bogomils held a moderate form which made the Devil, a fallen angel, ultimately dependent on God. They did, however, insist that the world had been created by the Devil, making matter, by definition, evil.

This view had a number of far-reaching consequences, breaking as it did from the Christian identification of God as the creator of the world: the miracles were interpreted allegorically, since Christ cannot have touched Devil-created matter; since matter cannot be the vehicle of grace, the sacraments were rejected, as were icons and feast days; the Cross was abhorred as the material instrument of Christ's murder, and the Virgin Mary paid no reverence; the Orthodox Church was considered false, while its liturgy and vestments were condemned. Only the Lord's Prayer was permitted and repeated eight times a day. It is interesting to note that, in the Bogomil version, 'daily bread' is translated as 'supersubstantial bread', also a legitimate translation from the Greek and one which did not associate the prayer with a material request.

The ethical teaching of the Bogomils – based on a rejection and renunciation of the world – aimed at union with God and avoidance of contact with matter. Marriage, with its possible consequence of the imprisonment of more souls in the material realm, was discouraged, as was the consumption of meat and wine; civil disobedience was promoted, a further thorn in the flesh of both ecclesiastical and secular authorities, made all the more uncomfortable by the great moral prestige of the Bogomil leaders. Obolensky sums this up by saying:

> In contrast to the intellectual and moral decadence of the clergy, who only too often left their flock without adequate support or

instruction, the Bogomils, owing to their saintly appearance, intimate knowledge of the Gospel, strict asceticism, ardent proselytism and courage in persecution, must have appeared to many Bulgarians as the true bearers of Christianity.[3]

Writing over 100 years later, Anna Comnena also accuses them of 'hypocrisy and pharisaic humility', saying that they are very clever at aping virtue, that their wickedness is hidden under the cloak and the cowl, that within they are uncontrollable wolves. Writing at the same time, the monk Euthymius Zigabenus gives an account of their doctrines and a description of the Bogomil initiation ceremony which one also finds, substantially unaltered, in Catharism. There are two degrees of initiation: 'Baptism of Christ through the Spirit', regarded as a more inward degree of baptism than with water; and what ultimately became the Cathar consolamentum. Zigabenus writes:

> Therefore they rebaptize those who come to them. First they appoint him [the catechumen] a period of confession, purification and intensive prayer. Then they lay the Gospel of St John on his head, invoke their Holy Spirit and sing the Lord's Prayer. After this Baptism they again set him a time for more rigorous training, a more continent life, purer prayer. Then they seek for proof as to whether he has observed these things and performed them zealously. If both men and women testify in his favour, they lead him to their celebrated consecration. They make the wretch face the East and again lay the Gospel on his . . . head. The men and women of the congregation place their foul hands on him and sing their unholy rite: this is a hymn of thanksgiving for his having preserved the impiety transmitted to him.[4]

If one cuts through the uncomplimentary epithets one can gain a good picture of the ceremony and the severe moral discipline which preceded it. After the first degree one joined the ranks of the 'believers' and after the second the 'elect' or 'perfect'. These distinctions of rank have a long history going back to early gnostic heresies which classified people into three groups: hylics, psychics and pneumatics. The hylics were materialists and sceptics, entirely uninterested in spiritual matters; the psychics had heard the call and begun some form of spiritual practice – their soul, *psyche*, was awakened; while the *pneumatikoi* had acquired the unitive insight associated with awareness of the spirit, the divine essence within and beyond form.

In the early Church, Clement of Alexandria gives the clearest exposition of the relationship between faith (*pistis*) and inner knowledge (*gnosis*).

> Faith then is a compendious knowledge of the essentials, but gnosis is a sure and firm demonstration of the things received through faith . . . carrying us on to unshaken conviction and certainty. . . . There seems to be a first kind of saving change from heathenism to faith, a second from faith to gnosis; and this latter, as it passes on into love, begins at once to establish a mutual friendship between that which knows and that which is known.[5]

It is clear that this inner spiritual knowledge or gnosis represents a stage beyond external acceptance of the Church's faith, pointing to an esoteric dimension of Christianity which has usually been consigned to heretic fringes. Mystics and Christian gnostics like Eckhart have been treated with deep suspicion, and Christianity has evolved more strongly as a religion of devotion (implying obedience) rather than one of spiritual understanding. The upsurge of interest in mystics like Eckhart indicates a thirst for a gnostic kind of insight. Writing on the subject of gnosis, the great philosopher, Frithjof Schuon, comments that 'the exoteric distinction between "the true religion" and "the false religion" is replaced, for the gnostic, by the distinction between gnosis and beliefs, or between essence and forms'.[6]

The Orthodox Church at the time of the Bogomils was clearly concerned with the first kind of distinction, while it seems that the Bogomil understanding was closer to the second. The popularity of Perennial Philosophy is one indication of the contemporary search for essence beyond form, gnosis beyond belief, principles beyond dogma. It was my own quest in this direction which brought me to Beinsa Douno in the first place.

The close connection between the Bogomils of Bulgaria and the Cathars of France is well established,[7] in terms of doctrines, rituals and habits. Steven Runciman highlights the fact that Cathar services strongly resembled the services of the early Christian Church up to the fifth century: the ritual feast was modelled on the communion feast and both ceremonies were terminated by a kiss of peace; the consolamentum was akin to the adult baptism of the early Church, which also insisted on a severe probationary period; 'finally, the actual ordination was identical, consisting of the laying on of hands and of the Gospel on the catechumen's head'. For complex political and social reasons these rigorous requirements were modified in the course of the fourth century but heretical sects continued to insist on moral and spiritual purification as an essential prerequisite to genuine baptism. In that sense the Bogomils and the Cathars were heirs to the esoteric disciplines of the early Church, making considerable spiritual demands on their followers and acting as a spur to reform within the Church itself.

This historical section can be appropriately closed with a Bogomil prayer:

> Cleanse me, my God,
> Purify me inwardly and outwardly,
> Purify Body, Soul and Spirit
> So that the seeds of light may grow within me
> And make me into a flaming torch.
> I should like to be my own flame
> So as to transform
> Everything in and around me
> Into Light.

Peter Deunov

In studying the history of religion Peter Deunov (Beinsa Douno) ascertained that no Master who came to earth was accepted: 'In all nations, without exception, they have been treated as traitors and liars.' He himself was persecuted by the Bulgarian clergy and accused, like Socrates, of corrupting the people: 'They stir the people up against me and say that I am defiling the name of God, that I am undermining the authority of the Holy Church. My question is: Where is your God? Where is the Son? The Son of God is the son of love. Where is your love? I can see no trace of love anywhere.'

In December 1922 the elders of the Church gathered to take action against Beinsa Douno. He commented that if they wanted to fight him they would have to fight with God.

What am I? A man who has come to earth to mislead all Bulgarians! With what powers do I manipulate? Do I have money? Do I have political influence? What are they afraid of? The fact that they are afraid of me indicates that I must have some power behind me which is terrifying to them. What is it? Supporting me is the Great Divine Love, the Great Divine Wisdom, the Great Divine Truth, the Great Divine Righteousness and Virtue. All living virtues support me. All wise and intelligent beings support me. Do you know how great they are?

People accused him of not attending church, to which he responded: 'My greatest misfortune is that I am always in the church; the church is the living people, their hearts.' The priests wondered why people came to him:

Why shouldn't they come! Society has fallen and I am supposed to be the cause. I don't want to interfere, but you yourselves should institute the reforms and plant the seeds of love. Let the church be filled with people, I would be happy if love reigned in the church. I would be even gladder if love would fill people's hearts.

He added:

I don't speak for worldly people but rather for those wise people, wherever they may be – in church, or in society – who serve God with love. Let them open their hearts and say to themselves: Lord God we serve Thee with love. Do with us what you will. This was Christ's teaching 2000 years ago, this is Christ's teaching today . . . Christ's teaching must be applied to life, at least to a certain extent, in the relations between fathers and mothers, sons and daughters, servants and masters; among all the people on earth. Let all priests and preachers come together and pray to God to help them apply Christ's teaching. When this comes to pass, peace will reign on earth.

In 1922 the annual August congress of the Brotherhood took place in Ternovo. One disciple arrived in town to find posters on the walls announcing an invitation by an Archbishop to hold a debate with Beinsa Douno; he was somewhat concerned, knowing that the Church did not take kindly to outsiders claiming to be messengers from God. The following day, the Orthodox Feast of the Transfiguration, the weather was magnificent and many people gathered outside the hall. Once inside, the Master asked his followers to give up their

seats to the numerous bishops and priests who had come with
a view to arguing with him. He began: 'The most important
thing in this world is life. My teaching does not consist of
theories and discussions. It is based on serious scientific
experiments.' It was striking that, from the start of the lecture,
many of the Orthodox audience gradually dozed off. Beinsa
Douno finished with these words:

> If I represent the conducting wire bringing the divine teaching and
> you cut that wire, what will you gain? You will lose your ideals
> like the Jews of 2000 years ago who rejected Christ's teaching.
> There will ultimately be no people on earth who will not bow
> before this truth and put it into practice. The sooner you
> Bulgarians accept this teaching, the better it will be for you.

The Orthodox audience woke up at this point and made no
critical remarks, to the surprise of the disciples. Then one of
them stood up and invited people to come back to the same
hall at two o'clock to hear the Archbishop's reply to, and
criticism of, Beinsa Douno's lecture. The Master then said:
'No! This meeting will not take place. At two o'clock no one
will be able to come here and those who are already here will
be unable to go out.' The disciples came out of the hall into
the bright sunshine and went back to the camp at midday,
wondering what could transpire to prevent the meeting.

At around one o'clock instructions came round the camp
for everyone to dig trenches round their tents, even though
there was no suggestion of rain in the calm blue sky. Then,
suddenly, huge clouds began to appear from all sides and a
ferocious wind arose, bending the trees right over and whirl-
ing leaves through the air. Large drops of rain began to fall,
followed by hail and torrential rain which began at two
o'clock and lasted until four. Naturally, nobody could venture
out of doors! The disciples commented that it was like witness-
ing a sacred ceremony taking place in nature.

When the rain had let up, those disciples who had remained
in town returned and reported that all those who had calum-
nied Beinsa Douno had been dumbfounded. The Master
explained the significance of the event, the moral being that
no one is in a position to hinder or destroy what God has
decided to do. He then gave one of his most moving songs
'Fir – Fur – Fen' ('Without Fear and Darkness'). The Master

'performed certain movements while singing it and filled it with a luminous power which overwhelmed our souls and evoked in us faith, courage and trust in a mighty world of light watching over us and leading us onward.' The next morning, quite a number of people came up from the town to listen to the Master and the bishops did not pursue their campaign any further at that stage.

THE LIFE OF THE MASTER BEINSA DOUNO

Peter Konstantinov Deunov was born on 12 July 1864, the youngest of three children of the priest, Konstantin Deunovski. He later adopted the spiritual name of Beinsa Douno, used among his followers in Bulgaria. 'I use a pseudonym', he said, 'so that no one knows who I am, they can only guess. Such a guess is not necessarily the truth.' Konstantin Deunovski was a prominent activist in the movement for the liberation of Bulgaria from five centuries of Turkish oppression. He held services and lessons in Bulgarian, developing the national sense of self-respect.

In his youth he had planned to become a monk and set off on a journey to Mount Athos with a small group of companions; they were shipwrecked on the return voyage. They landed at Tsayaz and went to Saloniki just before Easter 1854. The four young men entered the Church of Saint Dimitri on Good Friday afternoon and lit a candle of gratitude for having escaped from the shipwreck. On their way out they met an old priest who asked Konstantin to come back the next day for a private word. He returned at the same time on the Saturday and met the old priest, explaining his intention to become a monk.

After listening carefully to the young man's plans, the old priest told him that his salvation depended on his faith in Christ rather than on the place where he lived. Konstantin was struck by the halo above the old man's head and wondered for a moment whether the encounter was a reality or a dream. 'Your path is a different one,' the priest remarked. In the minutes which followed Konstantin became aware that providence had other plans for him than being a monk. At the end of the encounter the priest entrusted Konstantin with a sacred

Peter Deunov as a young man

document, predicted the end of the Turkish yoke and the recovery of the Bulgarian Church.

The meeting made a profound impression on Konstantin who changed course and committed his efforts to the liberation of Bulgaria which occurred twenty-four years later. A postscript to this story is suggested by an occasion on which Beinsa Douno asked his father the whereabouts of 'that book which I gave you in the church at that time' . . . but there is no reliable source for this anecdote.

Early years

Few details survive about Beinsa Douno's early years and education. One incident, though, shows an already developed allegorical understanding. He was talking with his older sister who was unhappy at the prospect of having to marry a man she did not like. Suddenly, a corn cob came crashing down from the rafter onto the floor and the grains of maize were scattered all over the place. Young Deunov turned to his sister and told her not to worry; she was not going to marry that man – 'Everything will disperse as the maize is dispersed on the floor.' This was indeed what happened.

Beinsa Douno received his secondary education in Varna and later at Svishtov. He learned to play the violin, a major aspect in his later teaching on music. He then taught for a period in the small village of Hatantsa before he left for the United States in August 1888. There he pursued his studies with a Methodist Institute of Theology and enrolled at the faculty of medicine in Madison, New England. He remained in America for seven years, returning in 1895.

Only a few reminiscences survive from these years. In 1920, an old lawyer happened to come into a bookshop run by one of Beinsa Douno's disciples. He lamented the fact that, had he so wished, the young Deunov's talents might have made him a millionaire. He also talked of student excursions during which Beinsa Douno had addressed the party on some unusual and beautiful topic, indicating to them the harmony and wisdom of the starry sky, the same qualities being present in the surrounding streams and flowers. He would sometimes distance himself from the group in order to pray or meditate. He would be totally absorbed and would tremble with surprise if anyone touched his shoulder; his face wore the expression of someone awakening from a deep and beautiful dream.

Another unusual incident is related by the writer, Grablashev, who was also studying in America at the time. He was asked to accompany Beinsa Douno on an excursion. They walked into the middle of a thick forest and eventually emerged into a wide meadow where a house stood next to a lake. The boatman rowed them over to the other side where they were met by a group of silent people who treated Beinsa Douno with great respect. The two were invited for refreshments and then taken to large hall in which a long table was placed with thirteen chairs around it. Eleven people sat round the table, along with the Master, leaving one chair vacant. Grablashev was warned not to ask any questions during the meeting and we have no record of the proceedings. After the meeting the two young men returned home. A few days later, Grablashev was curious to see if he could find the place again and set off on the route through the forest. Despite his best efforts he was quite unable to locate the meadow and lake. The mystery remains unsolved.

In 1895, on his return to Bulgaria, Beinsa Douno published his doctoral dissertation, *Science and Education*, and set about a systematic study of phrenology, an early science of head and facial features and their significance for character; he published five articles on the subject around the turn of the century. Much of his time, though, was spent in extended periods of seclusion in prayer and meditation. He speaks of this period in a letter:

> I am here working for the Lord. I am practising patience, with the help of good nature and kindness. I fill my heart with magnanimity and I strengthen it with disinterestedness and humility. I solicit the help of sincerity. I deck my forehead with courtesy, kindness and mercy. When I have finished this arduous task I shall bring the Lord God a choice offering and I shall thank Him for having extended His mercy to me in the fulfilment of my task, triumphing in His name. I shall thank Him for having placed me in a secure place within His habitation.

Another letter refers to the way he pursued his mission:

> Let us be true to the Divine Cause, and He will guide us. My prayer and ardent desire is to receive strength and inspiration from the Spirit who will teach us how to act in every circumstance: not according to human wisdom but according to God, not according to earthly laws but following the norms of Heaven.

Initiation

This inner preparation was essential for the Master to restore his link with the sublime higher world and with the Divine

Spirit. In March 1897 he experienced a first initiation in which he received instructions for his future work: he was chosen to be a Master for all humanity and would sow the seeds of a new culture of love. The spirit of an incarnated being realizes its unity with the primordial spirit. The Master called that day, 'the day of the accomplishment of the promise of the Lord'.

Shortly after this initiation, Beinsa Douno began work on *The Testament of the Colour Rays* which was eventually published in 1912. He read the Bible several times, pondering on the deep meaning of key passages and arranging them to correspond with the development of virtues and the colours associated with them. Quotations were classified according to colours and the spirits of, for instance, love, life, promise, wisdom, truth, power and grace. The spirit of Christ corresponds to the white and diamond rays, the light of the world. The book is one of the few published which was actually written by the Master himself.

In October 1898 the Master delivered an extraordinary proclamation – A Call to My People – to a small society in Varna. It was twenty years after Bulgaria's liberation. Listen, he said, to the words of heaven:

> I have come from above on the command of God, your Heavenly Father, who has assigned me the mission of warning you to turn away from the evil path and to preach to you the truth of life which comes from the heavenly dwellings of eternal light, a truth which will enlighten every mind, renew every heart, and uplift and refresh every spirit. You are the chosen children of truth who were preordained to form the seed of the new humanity of which Slavdom as a family, descendants of Judah, will become the hearth.

'The revival of a nation', he continued,

> requires a harmony between the heart and mind; they must proceed parallel to love and virtue, as power and reason together guide and maintain the path of their good aspirations. Everything outside these conditions is hopelessly lost. . . . I have arrived in this decaying world at a very important moment to assert the necessary influence, to lead you away from this wild path towards which the nations of the world are mindlessly rushing.

Peter Deunov around 1920

Brotherhood of Light

In 1900, Beinsa Douno instituted the Fellowship of Light and held its first convention on 6 April in Varna. Outwardly, it was an insignificant affair; inwardly, it corresponded to the sowing of a small grain of wheat in fertile soil. Only three disciples attended; one of these asked during a lecture why the others had not arrived on time! The Master later explained:

Now you are only three people. But you will be many. The hall is not empty. The chairs are occupied by invisible beings. Today is the first convention of the White Brotherhood in Bulgaria. Now you are only three men, but you will become thousands.

This did indeed come about: the number of his followers was estimated at some 40,000 at the time of his death and in the 1930s there were 144 study-circles around the country.

In the succeeding years Beinsa Douno travelled the length and breadth of Bulgaria teaching and healing while acquainting himself more intimately with the characteristics of the Bulgarian people. He encouraged their strivings, writing to one disciple: 'I am praying earnestly that God may illuminate you and bless you more abundantly, that you may receive the Spirit of God who will bind us in a closer spiritual unity, that we may carry in our soul and heart His great unspeakable love.' He advised them:

The Boundless One is always true,
And His Love is unchangeable.
Listen to His silent voice within you
And to His instructions.
The Will of God is that you grow strong in His Love.
The Boundless One will bring His cause
To a perfect completion.
Practise constancy, wise patience, pure-heartedness,
With clarity of mind, a sound soul and a vigorous spirit.

At that early stage a few of his older disciples were uncertain about the powers and mission of the Master. During a meeting, when he was due to give a lecture, one of these older people made a remark to the effect that they, too, knew about spiritual subjects – perhaps Beinsa Douno had simply read and remembered a little more than they had and was no different from them.

Shortly afterwards the Master entered with a smile and looked around. He then took the key, locked the door and placed the key on the table. No sooner had he sat down in his seat than he vanished. The next thing his astonished hearers knew was that the Master was outside the door knocking and asking whether they could hear him. After a while he reappeared in his seat, saying, 'Here I am again in front of you.'

He then disappeared again, knocking at the door, 'Now I am outside again.' He became visible once more in the room, 'Now I am sitting with you again.' The exercise was repeated a third time. When calm had been restored, the Master said: 'Remember, I am with you and among you, but I am not like you.'

There are many anecdotes which illustrate the extraordinary capacities of the Master. One of his disciples was a train driver who once fell asleep at the controls of his train. Just before arriving at a station where he was meant to stop, the driver was suddenly awoken by the train's whistle. He was quite amazed to see the Master standing next to him pressing the button for the whistle which announced the arrival of the train! He was just about to address a word of thanks to the Master when he disappeared.

A poor widow found herself in dire straits with children to feed and no prospect of any improvement in her circumstances. She decided to poison herself in order to put an end to her misery. All of a sudden, a man whom she did not know came into her flat and removed the glass, saying, 'What are you doing, and why do you wish to die?' The widow described her situation whilst the man listened attentively. He comforted her and finally told her that her situation would improve. She decided not to take her life and soon after this mysterious encounter found a job which enabled her to feed her children. One day she happened to find herself at Izgrev, the Centre of the Brotherhood, when, to her complete astonishment, she recognized in the Master the person who had expeditiously arrived and dissuaded her from poisoning herself.

Another story concerned a Bulgarian worker who had gone to America with a view to earning a lot of money; he left his wife and children in Bulgaria. After a while he finally married another woman in America and resolved never to return to Europe. His first wife, however, continued to write to him expressing her despair at his prolonged absence and begging him to return. She received no reply. One day she had a personal interview with the Master who listened to her plight and told her not to worry; her husband would return. From that day the husband began receiving visits from an old man with a beard and long white hair. This stranger spoke to him insistently, telling him that his wife and children were expecting him in Bulgaria. At first the worker did not wish to listen but the man returned every day with the same message. In the end he resolved to take a steamer back to Bulgaria. He was greatly surprised to meet the same old man on the boat! The man never tired of repeating his message. The manifestations only ceased when he reached home. He told his wife the story; she guessed that the old man must have been a materialization of the Master. Any doubts she might have entertained were dispelled when the husband himself visited Izgrev. He spotted the Master in the distance and exclaimed, 'There is the man who made me come back to Bulgaria!' When they were introduced, the husband was anxious to know if the Master had recently been in America. Smilingly, he replied that he had not been there for some considerable time.

The Teaching Mission

From 1905 to 1926, Beinsa Douno was based in the Bulgarian capital, Sofia, at 66 Opalchenska Street, where he gave his early lectures. Sometimes there was not enough room in the house and he was obliged to talk at the window, so that both those inside and outside were able to hear. The people attending often found the answers to their immediate preoccupations in some part of the talk. Beinsa Douno spoke softly but clearly, occasionally prefacing his talks with songs composed by himself and played on the violin. These songs were written down and, together with the melodies, number some 200. He encouraged his disciples to sing every day. Nowadays songs are always sung at meetings and summer camps in the mountains.

From 1914 onwards, the lectures were all taken down in shorthand before being transcribed and edited for publication. He gave some 7000 lectures in the subsequent thirty years, two thirds of these appearing in a series of some 150 volumes in Bulgarian. This represents an even larger output than his prodigious contemporary, Rudolf Steiner.

In 1922, the Master opened what he called his Occult School, a term which might better be rendered in English as

Esoteric. There were two classes, a General Class whose lectures took place at 5 am on Wednesdays and Fridays; and a Special Class for Young People at 5 am on Fridays. The two classes had different aims: the Special Class was especially rich in instructions and exercises, with a view to the developing energies of young people. They needed a good direction and a favourable atmosphere for their growth. The General Class recognized that adults had already travelled a part of their journey and had mistakes and habits to correct and reform. Both classes, however, were exercises in applying the insights gained to life itself, training the mind, heart and will in the process:

> The challenge of the divine school is to prepare the minds and hearts of people to apply the Truth. One of the qualities of the great school of life – the school of the White Brotherhood or the so-called Divine School – is that one puts to the test all that one learns. Theory and practice go hand in hand in this school. It shows the disciple not only the way to the Truth, but also its application.

All the lectures began punctually at that early hour and the most intensive period of study was between the autumn and spring equinoxes. During the spring and summer lectures were followed by gymnastic exercises and paneurhythmy while, during the months of July and August from the mid-1920s, summer camps were established in the Rila mountains. Lectures took place on the Mount of Prayer or on the summit of Moussala after sunrise at 5 am. On Sundays at 10 o'clock there was a general lecture open to everyone; this was usually prefaced by a quotation from the Gospel. Like the Bogomils, the Master was particularly fond of Saint John.

The 1920s saw the establishment of the Brotherhood Centre on the outskirts of Sofia. It was called Izgrev, meaning Sunrise. By 1926, the building work was sufficiently advanced for the annual congress to proceed in spite of the reluctance of the authorities. The midday meal was always vegetarian and communal; townspeople were welcome to come and share it. On occasion even Communists would turn up. There is a delightful anecdote concerning one such comrade who was sceptical of the Master's claims and asked whether he could tell him something known only to himself. The Master thought

Peter Deunov (Beinsa Douno) at prayer

for a moment before informing the man that he always rattled metal against the contribution box without ever putting any coins into it. The man's embarrassment testified to the accuracy of the observation.

Congresses were traditionally held in August and were transferred to the sacred Rila mountains from 1929. From around 1920, Beinsa Douno began to bring his disciples into closer contact with nature by encouraging them to meet the sunrise and organizing excursions to Mount Vitosha near Sofia and to Moussala. The first three-day excursion was memorable in a number of respects, according to survivors. First of all there was no ski lift to climb the 3000 feet from the base and then no one had either tents or sleeping bags. The weather was atrocious for most of the period as it still can be in the middle of August. It was a real initiation in both physical and spiritual senses. The first camps also involved rising before 3.30 am in order to climb the 1800 feet to Moussala; the ascent was a spiritual and physical exercise to strengthen the will, but disciples were rewarded by the extraordinary spectacle of sunrise from the peak. It was, and is, in the mountains that the most intensive spiritual work is performed. The camps give everyone an opportunity to live as brothers and sisters in a supportive atmosphere of mutual aid.

Advice and healing

Many people came to Beinsa Douno for advice, help and healing. He said of illnesses that 'they are an educative method by which nature balances the energies of the organism. A sick person merged with Divine Love can become healthy in a moment.' The Master recommended the natural therapeutic methods of food, air, water and light. He sometimes advised disciples to raise their thoughts and feelings to a higher plane by prayer and fasting: 'Purity of thoughts, feelings, desires and the body is a condition for health. Always live and move in love.'

One of the disciples employed at the post office had the sudden misfortune to see his wife fall gravely ill. He wrote to the

Master asking advice on medical care and left for work with the letter in his pocket. On installing himself at his desk he noticed a telegram personally addressed to him. He quickly opened it and was astounded to find that it was from the Master giving him all the necessary instructions for his wife. The letter was still in his pocket. He followed the advice and his wife soon got better.

The mother of one of the secretaries fell ill with a gastric complaint which closed down the normal functions of her intestines. The best doctors in Sofia were called upon to no avail. The secretary went to see the Master who asked whether her mother was a believer. She replied that she was indeed, so he advised: 'Don't worry, keep calm. When you return home, open your Bible and read your mother some of the psalms, whatever you happen to chance upon.' She followed these instructions which had a calming effect on herself and her sister, as well as on the mother. They also discovered that the mother knew several by heart and joined in the recitation. Her distress was relieved within the hour and everything returned to normal within a few days. Reflecting on this cure, the secretary supposed that the Master had brought the power of thought to bear on the situation, transforming negative states into positive ones.

In January 1938 a disciple was working in a provincial town when he noticed a swelling in his left eye which gradually worsened and turned blue. He went to consult three oculists but their treatments made no impression. He was very worried and resolved to go back to Sofia to consult the Master. He arrived at 10 o'clock one morning. The Master said that he was in great danger of going blind, made him sit down, and passed his hands several times in front of the eyes. The disciple then went outside into the garden and fell asleep. On waking up he felt that his head was free again and looked at his eye in a pocket mirror. It was almost normal: the swelling had gone down, it had reopened and the blue colour had disappeared. After two or three days there was no trace of the infection.

One young disciple suffered a particularly acute bout of appendicitis and his father wanted to proceed with an operation. The disciple refused, convinced that the Master would save him. One Friday morning, between 5 and 6 o'clock, the state of the patient deteriorated; he practically lost consciousness. During this time the Master was in the middle of giving a lecture. He suddenly paused and seemed to look into the distance. He interrupted the lecture and quickly went up to his room where he poured a certain liquid into a glass and rushed off to the patient's home. He emptied the contents of the glass into the patient's mouth and went back to the lecture. The patient later said that he had drunk something like liquid fire which brought on profuse sweating – the sheets had to be changed fourteen times! He was completely cured after a few days' rest.

A friend of a disciple was a wealthy industrialist who fell ill and could no longer fulfil his business obligations. After a year's treatment, which had no effect whatsoever, his colleagues decided to sack him and cut off his salary. This threw the man into complete despair. Another disciple explained the situation to the Master who replied: 'Can he make a gift of a large sum to help the poor, to provide them with indispensable material goods which they are deprived of – food, clothing, heating, etc? If he is prepared to do this, he can let me know.' The patient did make a substantial gift. The Master was notified and ordered the friend to buy some black radishes, to press them and make a teacup's worth of juice which should then be heated and administered to the patient. These instructions were followed. He felt a good deal better the next day and was completely cured after a few more days of such treatment. Seeing the success of the remedy, the friend asked whether it could be given to other people. The Master replied that it would have no effect on other people and that it would not have been effective in this case if the patient had not been prepared to make a considerable sacrifice. He added: 'People should know that every good which you desire on earth has a high price.'

One of the most spectacular cases of healing was related by two student disciples. They were on their way back to Sofia in the train and were being taunted on account of their long hair, at that time a sign that they belonged to the Brotherhood. Another passenger, a lieutenant-colonel, suddenly got up and told their oppressors that he would throw them out of the window if they continued to make fun of the Master. He also reproached the two disciples for not standing up for themselves.

He then told them that he had a daughter who had suc-
cumbed to tuberculosis; she was their only child. They
consulted specialists in Bulgaria, but also in Austria, Switzer-
land and Germany, all to no avail; there was no help and no
hope. They therefore came back home so that their daughter
could die in peace. Her state deteriorated; she was semi-
conscious and was eating no food; her days were numbered.
The parents then decided to kill themselves as soon as the
daughter had died. It was then that the colonel heard about
the Master, so he went to see him. He fell on his knees while
he explained the desperate situation, and exclaimed: 'Master,
you helped that Roman centurion, and cured his daughter
with a word. I beg you, Master, help me too!' The Master
looked kindly at the man and said: 'Get up! Go back home!
Your daughter is saved!'

The man went back home and was thunderstruck to find his
daughter sitting up doing embroidery, rather than on her
deathbed as he had left her. Her mother was in the process of
frying some bread for her daughter to eat. When he questioned
his wife more closely about the moment their daughter had felt
better and regained her appetite, he reckoned that it was
precisely the moment when he had fallen on his knees in front
of the Master and implored his help.

The foregoing anecdotes could be multiplied many times, but
they give an impression of the variety of ways in which Beinsa
Douno treated people and of the meaning of the illness in
any particular context. Even if he always intervened at the
critical moment, he often demanded a supreme effort from the
patient. A paralysed man, for example, was told to go out and
dig his garden; he replied that he could not even lift the hoe,
still less use it. But the Master insisted: he needed to make an
effort of will. The paralysed man took the advice and gradually became better.

Later teachings

Throughout the 1930s and early 1940s the Master continued
to lecture systematically throughout the year. Summer camps
were held near Moussala and in the region of the Seven Lakes.

Visitors began to arrive from abroad and more than 500 people attended the last pre-war camp in 1939. At one of the camps near Moussala, the Master gave a memorable address after everyone had come down from the peak in the fog and rain. It was entitled 'The Small Blade of Grass'. The fog hung low over the lake and the grass was bent under the heavy moisture. The Master always looked for the creative side of a difficult situation:

> Every blade coming out of the ground will see the sun. You may ask now why we are sitting in this rain. The rain is an object-lesson for us. When the field is sown, the rain is a blessing. When the field is not sown, the rain is a misfortune. Why were we met on Moussala by thunder, rain and snow? This was the language of heaven. God says: 'Tell these people that if they do My will, My blessing shall rest upon them.' It is a beautiful thing to accomplish the will of God – always to be good.
>
> Many of you have not yet manifested your virtues. That is to say: many of your seeds have not yet put forth a blade in your field. Why did I bring you to Moussala? To know God! He speaks to you from above, but you do not understand His language. He says to you: 'You must love one another.' To love as people love perverts you. You must love as God loves. You will love and forgive. For whom should you work? Only for God. This thought 'For God' must always be in your mind. Whatever you do, do it only for God.
>
> If anyone asks me, 'Why do you love and serve God?' I shall say, 'Because God loves me.' Service and work are always the way to respond to love. Love works. Know this! It is Moussala – the high peak. Good is something inner. People must be good in their hearts. The good which God has deposited in you should be developed by your working solely for God. You will struggle until your virtues take the upper hand and say, 'I can serve God at all times and under all conditions.'
>
> You say, 'Let us be good.' There are three categories of being good. One can be good for oneself, or one can be good for one's neighbour. But I consider the ideal state that of being good for God. People have learned the art of being good for themselves. They also know how to be good for their neighbour. From now on we are to learn the art of being good for God.
>
> Consider the small bee which flies long distances to gather pollen and prepare honey. Is it not good for itself and its neigh-bour? Yes indeed. But the bee has not learned or understood the great law of being good for God. Try to take some of its honey

Peter Deunov teaching

and it will immediately sting you. The bee does not give anything for God. It has arranged its life excellently. Its house is fine, its body is clean, it is industrious, but it does not know the law that it must be good for God. We are also like the bees. We are very good for our houses and our neighbours, but as far as God is concerned, if anything is required of us, we immediately show Him our sting.

From now on you will learn the law of being good for God. That is the greatest thing. When you learn it, your whole life will acquire a new meaning – living nature will begin to speak to you and you will study it. Now I shall give each of you, as a souvenir, a blade of grass. It will be an emblem for you. This blade of grass will be an image for you of the idea of 'serving God'. Serving God is the great science of life. When I speak to you of serving God, I mean that sacred moment of our soul when we approach God in our purity and perfection. Pure and bright in our thoughts, desires and actions! Only in that state of perfection of Spirit and purity of soul can we understand the divine science which will teach us what our souls crave and our Spirit strives for. When we begin to serve God, we need divine knowledge – the knowledge of living nature.

After that talk, one of the disciples said: 'Master, how good it would be if you could always be with us and speak to us thus!'.

The Master answered: 'There has been no time when I have not been with you.'

Then another person said: 'How good it is for us to remain here!'

The Master answered: '"Here" means "with God" and we shall always be with God.'

The Last Days

During his last years, Beinsa Douno wanted to pay a final visit to his beloved Moussala and asked Boyan Boev to organize the expedition. The problem was to obtain a car for the journey, as both petrol and cars were in short supply. Another disciple volunteered to get the necessary permission. It turned out that one could only obtain a car for an ill person, so the disciple used the pretext of another friend's sore foot to obtain a car. He rushed back to Izgrev but the Master said: 'I am not going to travel in a car that has been taken by a lie.' The disciple went back to the chief official and had no difficulty in obtaining a car, simply by saying that the Master wanted to go to Moussala. The three-day excursion was profoundly moving as the Master knew that he would not be visiting Moussala again in the physical body. He walked slowly and often stopped to survey his surroundings. He looked up at the high peaks in the sun, breathed the fragrant air of the pines. He stopped at bridges and contemplated the crystalline water.

The war was a difficult time for the whole of the Bulgarian people. In January 1944, after the bombing of Sofia, the Master moved to Marchaevo near Mount Vitosha. He was aware that favourable conditions for his work were going to be curtailed.

In October Methodi Konstantinov visited him. The Master announced: 'I have accomplished my task on the earth. I am going to leave.' A few days before his departure in December, Konstantinov visited him again. He said to them: 'What is Beethoven, what is Jesus, what is Deunov? It is only God who is eternal and boundless, only God is a reality.' Then he quietly began to sing 'Aoum', making beautiful gestures: it was the last song he sang on earth.

The short, cold, foggy days of December seemed, according to Konstantinov, to be symbols of what was happening in their souls. One day he passed the Master's room. He got up and came to the door, whispering in his ear, 'Methodi, go away, the physical body is something unabiding, transitory – millions of bodies remained on the battlefields.' The Master was withdrawing into himself. Methodi asked him whether he was going to stay a little longer in the physical world. He looked at him and made a negative gesture.

Among the last words of the Master were the following:

> It is only with and through love that the world will be set to rights. For my part, I am leaving. My work will continue on the other side. You do not have much time left. Be vigilant and do not be discouraged. You must all progress with greater enthusiasm. Be sincere and true to your mission. May peace be with you. A small task has been completed.

The Master was diagnosed as having double pneumonia and breathed his last at 6 o'clock on the morning of 27 December. His body was dressed in a white suit and laid out in the lecture hall at Izgrev. The disconsolate disciples sang songs to the accompaniment of the violin and harp. On the 28th, Maria Zlateva recalls that she was playing the violin with Acen Aranoudov on the harp and Katia Griva singing gently. In front of them was a table with a bowl of fruit on top. They played with hearts heavy with grief. All of a sudden an apple fell out of the bowl, rolled down and stopped at Acen's feet. Then another fell and went to Katya. Finally, a third one came to Maria herself: 'It seemed that someone was pushing them down with his fingers. We fell silent. We bent down and picked up the apples. We were grateful to the Master that he showed us his love and appreciation.'

Two days after the Master's death, the Communist authorities came to Izgrev to arrest him. But he had already left. They would certainly have detained him and probably executed him. This visit marked the beginning of a forty-five-year period of harassment and persecution which only lifted in the autumn of 1989. The doctor who performed the post mortem said that he had never encountered such a virgin organism in fifty years of practice. The disciples obtained special permission from the Communist chief, Georgi Dimitrov, to have his body buried in the garden. Although Izgrev itself was demolished and, ironically, the Soviet Embassy erected on the site, the garden has survived. The headstone bears no name: only a Pentagram inscribed 'Love, Wisdom, Truth, Equity, Virtue' on the five sides.

On 27 March 1945 a small group of disciples met in the lecture hall at Izgrev to read a lecture, sing and pray. The eyes of those present were directed towards the Master's vacant chair, a chair which was by no means empty for Pacha Theodorova, one of the stenographers. She saw the spiritual image of the Master sitting in the chair, assuming a position characteristic for the end of a lecture. She wondered at first whether it was an illusion, but no, it was undoubtedly the image of the Master, surrounded by a brilliant light. The impression lasted for some time, and could therefore be studied in detail. The light which surrounded him was made up of rays of various lengths and emanating in different directions. Others, too, experienced similar visions: sometimes his face shone like a sun while, on other occasions, intense luminous rays emanated from his whole spiritual body. Such reports continue to this day and indicate the Master's continuing presence and activity.

THE MISSION OF THE MASTER BEINSA DOUNO

Communications and the comparative study of religions, among other things, have revolutionized the mutual understanding of distinct spiritual traditions. It is easy to forget that, for many peoples of the Third World, Christianity was itself part of the imperialist cultural package exported by western Europe. Other religions were considered to be inferior, if not actually barbaric. The philosopher Schopenhauer was one of the first to appreciate the Upanishads, then came the great work of F. Max Muller who compiled the fifty-volume edition of *The Sacred Books of the East*. Early anthropologists such as Sir Edward Tylor, Sir J.G. Frazer and Andrew Lang revealed patterns of the religious imagination. William James delivered his epoch-making Gifford Lectures, The Varieties of Religious Experience, in 1901–2, inaugurating a new attitude to mystical experience. C.G. Jung uncovered hidden depths in the human psyche. Eastern sages, following in the footsteps of Ramakrishna and Vivekananda, brought their wisdom to the West; their efforts were paralleled by the work of the Theosophical Society. Out of the latter sprang the anthroposophy of Rudolf Steiner.

At the same time the rigid dogmas of traditional Christianity were scrutinized by biblical scholars and eroded by a scepticism emanating from scientific discoveries in biology, astronomy and geology; all of this was reinforced by emerging political and philosophical materialism which rejected religious intuitions as outmoded superstition. But the human soul and spirit abhors a vacuum, a theme taken up by the great scholar of religions, Mircea Eliade, and by the school of perennial philosophers. These included René Guenon, Titus Burckhardt, Frithjof Schuon and S.H. Nasr. The materialist outlook simply does not correspond to our deepest aspirations and inner realities: we need a philosophy that transcends the outer limitations of physical science and the inner restrictions of fundamentalist religion. This is what I believe is offered by the teaching of Master Beinsa Douno, an esotericism which has its roots firmly within the western spiritual tradition.

In 1914, the Master spent a part of the summer in a small village called Arbanassi where he spent a long period in solitude, fasting and prayer. One day, when he was on a mountain top nearby, Christ appeared to him and said: 'Give me your body, your heart and your mind and work for me.' The Master answered: 'Lord, may Thy will be done. I am ready.'

This was not the Master's only encounter with Christ, as he said: 'Someone asked me: Do you know Christ? I know Him, I speak to Him. Many times I have conversed with Him.' Or again: 'I have seen Christ. I know Him well, I have conversed with Him. I have found no better teaching than Christ's, nor a language which is better than His. This teaching embraces everything. What did Christ teach? He taught love. I teach love too. Christ said about Himself that He is the Son of God, therefore you too may call yourselves sons of God.'

Christ, for Beinsa Douno, is the first manifestation and limitation of God as love. He brought a new life and force to the earth and was the turning point between the process of involution and evolution of consciousness. The fundamental injunctions of Christ were to love God, to love one's neighbour, and to love one's enemy. It is not hard to see that humanity as a whole is not yet ready to apply these principles given 2000 years ago. 'When', asks Beinsa Douno,

> have people ever accepted a truth at the time it was revealed to them? Did not Christ bring a great truth into the world? What did they do to Him? After Him came the Apostles, they too were persecuted. This is how they have received the men who have introduced new ideas in the fields of science, religion and government. No matter how good they may have been, they have been rejected.
>
> Many people are expecting Christ to be born again in the flesh. If Christ is to be born again, it is in your souls that He must be born. You cannot expect Christ to be born of a woman. When He is born in your soul, that is the resurrection, that is the awakening of the human soul. And when He comes to live in people, they will all be alive indeed. Christ is in the world today. You want to see Him in form but if He fills your hearts with the best feelings, what more can you ask for? Is that not He?

The Master often stressed the continuity of his teaching with that of Christ. He said:

> You must realize that I have been sent by God, that I have not come merely because of my own desire. I am sent by God to work for the coming of the Kingdom of God on earth. God speaks through Christ. God speaks through me.

The ideas which I am introducing in my lectures are taken from a divine source. That which Christ spoke, and that which I say come from the same source.

I have come to reveal love, to bring love down to earth. This is my mission.

We preach the Christ of Love, which supports and fills every heart; we preach the Christ of Wisdom, which illuminates every mind; we preach the Christ of Truth, which liberates and elevates the world.

I preach the Christian teaching as we must apply it in our lives; I wish to show you what Christianity consists of. I am in favour of the Kingdom of God, because we are Sons of God, and the Sons of God are those who wish to serve God and humanity through love, honestly and without deceit.

Beinsa Douno described his creed as follows:

I believe in love and wisdom which have created life. I believe that they have the power to recreate the world. I believe that the living love and wisdom can change our life, our society and our homes. When we accept love and wisdom, truth and righteousness will come. The angels will descend from heaven and plant good fruits in our souls.

I say to you: God lives in me and I live in God. If you don't believe that, it won't hurt me.

You ask me what I want, and why I came to earth. I want to light up the extinguished lanterns and make you shine either like candles or lamps or a torch.

I don't preach salvation to you. I preach how to fulfil the will of God on earth. I teach the way of fulfilling the will of the living God in whom your liberation is hidden. He will make you feel like brothers and sisters to each other, preparing you for the great life which is coming to earth. It is not necessary to be enchanted by my speeches or my person. It is important that you accept the teaching, applying it to solve all your problems.

He added:

It is not important who I am. It is important how much you profit from me. Thank God that you have found a source which flows, and of my part, say nothing of it.

We are called 'Deunovists'. This is a mistake. I am not a Deunovist myself. I preach the love of God. Do not say that the teaching I preach was invented by a certain Deunov, but say that it is the teaching of the Fellowship of Light. Tomorrow someone else will come, with another name. The greatness of all those who have come into the world consists in the fact that they have transmitted the truth given to them by God.

If you imagine that you can separate the Master from God and God from the Master, you do not understand the laws. If the Master thinks he can do something outside God, he is on the wrong track. The only Master who teaches people is God. In order to do so, He takes on one form or another. This is what makes God sometimes visible and sometimes invisible.

Do not follow me but rather God's love. There is something unusual in the world and that is the divine. It is the divine that I want you to know and come to understand. In order to be able to understand it, you must enter the Kingdom of Love. With a firm footing in the ground of love, know that He who has created the world will never betray you. Have absolute faith in God.

The teaching I am bringing to earth is not mine. It is a divine teaching, it is God's teaching. It is not my own thought, it is a divine thought. It predates the creation of the world and is therefore a manifestation of ourselves. Even the smallest impulse towards the Good is the language of God.

I am often asked what is the teaching which I am preaching. I answer: it is the teaching of living nature which includes in itself all living power with which science concerns itself. It is the science of man, the science of what is rational in the world. It is the science of God, of love.

Beinsa Douno never tired of stressing the crucial future importance of love:

Love is necessary for the rescuing of the world. It is the only force which can bring peace between the nations, each of which has a mission to accomplish on earth. Love is beginning to appear; goodness, justice and light will triumph; it is simply a question of time. The religions need to be purified; they all contain something divine, but this has been obscured by the repeated addition of human conceptions. All believers will have to get together and agree on one single principle: to make love the basis of any and every belief. Love and brotherhood, that is the common basis.

Two of the most important symbols in Beinsa Douno's teaching are the spring or source and the grain of wheat. God is the supreme source and life which brings about germination. The words of the Master, elaborations of Love, Wisdom and

Truth, are food and drink to hungry and thirsty souls; they also help bring about the germination of those latent divine qualities which lie deep within us. The seeds which this prophet for our times planted in Bulgaria in the first half of this century are just now emerging out of the dark earth. The first shoots of the new culture are beginning to sprout and will bear fruit in the fullness of time.

The Master had no wish for his followers to preach the divine teaching in a propagandist manner. He described his teaching as a meal which people could come and eat, assimilating what they could. One final anecdote illustrates his preferred approach. An ardent disciple came to him asking advice on how to spread the good news of love. He thought of procuring a soap box on which to preach, but Beinsa Douno said: 'No, not like that! These are outdated methods which have not succeeded in the past! There are other methods.'

On enquiring further, Beinsa Douno asked him whether he had ever breathed the mountain air fragrant with violets. Yes, indeed he had. 'Then', continued the Master,

> you must have breathed this marvellous perfume without seeing the violets. You might then have discovered the little flowers which were sending you their perfume hidden under some shrub. That is how we work, like the violets. Our radiant thoughts, our noble feelings, as well as our useful and unselfish actions are like the perfume of the violets. If you meet a questing soul, just say a couple of words. Light a little sacred flame and leave it. This may seem an insignificant deed, but because this soul is connected to other souls, they too will be illumined. Such is the law.

> The perfecting of Love will be the aim of my life.
> Perfect love removes all fear from the soul,
> And brings peace and joy to the spirit.
>
> In the fulfilment of the Will of God
> Lies the power of the human soul.

Notes

1. Runciman, S. *The Medieval Manichee*, Cambridge University Press, 1947, p. 67; Obolensky, D. *The Bogomils*, Hall, 1948, p. 117.
2. Obolensky, op. cit., p. 121.
3. ibid., p. 141.
4. ibid., pp. 215-6.
5. Churton, T. *The Gnostics*, Weidenfeld & Nicolson, 1987, p. 41.
6. Schuon, F. *Gnosis*, Perennial Books, 1959, p. 82.
7. Runciman, op. cit. p. 163.

For the quotations from Beinsa Douno, I have used translations from the French and a good many unpublished manuscripts.

— 1 —

God

For many people, God is just a concept in which they believe or disbelieve. For Beinsa Douno, as for mystics in all traditions, God is an immediate reality, the innermost principle of Love, Wisdom and Truth, the very being of the universe and of life. He uses various terms to describe God: the Primordial Principle, Ultimate Reality, the Sun of Life, manifesting as light in our minds, warmth in our hearts and strength in our wills.

In an age of doubt and rational scepticism which has systematically denied the existence of God, Beinsa Douno advanced a new and arresting 'proof' by stating that the existence of love implies the existence of God. Love is an inner quality; God can only be found by looking into the depths within, by stilling the chattering distractions of the mind. We have all been touched by love in some form; this is to be touched by God. We ourselves are transmitters and instruments of Divine Love, not its creators. When we love or are beloved, this is a divine exchange of love. Beinsa Douno insists on the importance of making the divine connection by maintaining an awakened consciousness. This link is also sustained through gratitude.

Many contemporaries deny the existence of God because of the great suffering they experience or see around them, even though much of it is human in origin, the result of the exercise of human freedom. We do not have a profound enough philosophy of suffering, especially if we consider that the object of life is happiness rather than growth. The rose and the vine suffer through pruning, the seed is buried in the dark earth and loses its life. Beinsa Douno characterizes the path of suffering as the path to God in that it awakens us from our slumbers and encourages us to work consciously, to pass from the death of winter through to the resurrection of spring.

No one can pretend that this process is easy or painless; it requires great courage and perseverance:

> Only through trials and tribulations does one come to understand the true nature of love, faith and hope. Only in this way does one understand that love is stronger than lack of love, than hell and death; that faith is stronger than doubt; that hope is stronger than despair; that good is stronger than evil.

Help, though, is never far away, as many have discovered when they pray in moments of supreme anguish. We are never completely abandoned, even if we feel desolate and bleak within, for God is the ultimate resource and resort living in the depths of our being. Beinsa Douno gives the following formula for those feeling uneasy or disturbed: 'I live in a world of perfect harmony. I am surrounded by intelligent and elevated beings from the higher world, who are constantly ready to assist me.'

> Do not look for God outside yourself, for the God you seek
>   does not exist.
> God manifests in us as light in our spirit,
> Sweet warmth in our heart,
> And strength in our will.
> Look within for the living God, and be thankful.

> Ask that God may live in you, that He may manifest
>   through you.
> Only God can transform human beings.
> Everyone seeks the meaning of life.
> The meaning of life lies in communion with God.

•   •   •

God is love, God is love, God is love, love, love
Eternal, without bounds, full of life,
Life of the kindly Spirit of God,
Spirit of kindness, Spirit of holiness,
Spirit of complete peace and joy
For every soul, for every soul. (1)

God is the sun of life. When this sun awakens, you will see
and understand the world in the right way. (2)

No matter in what phase of life one may be, whether
young, adult or old, whether rich or poor, learned or
ignorant, we must be awakened. Who must awaken us?
God must do this. Why? Because God is the sun of life.
When this sun awakens a person, it will open their eyes in
order that they may see and understand the world aright
and work in it. (3)

God is ultimate reality. The sun is the expression of God.
The spirit is the inward bond of things. (4)

God is everywhere: in the light, in the warmth, in the air,
in the water. He is in every good thought, in every good
feeling and in every noble deed. (27X)

God is light, while light is the means through which God
sends life to the world. (106X)

Light comes from God. It illumines the path of every
human being. Everyone should love God since they receive
light from Him. (5)

It is written in the Gospel 'God is love'. The love of God
brings knowledge and freedom. (4)

We have to love so that we may find God – because
He is love. (93X)

A person whose heart has not been filled with love does
not know God. (85X)

When you go out into the world, be careful lest you
should stumble and extinguish your candle. Many people
think that it is possible to be without a candle, i.e. without
God – that is why they deny Him. (87X)

Do not assert or deny the existence of God, but let Him live within you. (64X)

When God comes to live within you, everything that torments you, discourages you and makes you discontented will disappear. True happiness will come and you will say, 'Now I really understand everything. Now I understand that God lives within me.' (85X)

Work for God with love. He does not want you to work for Him without love. The blessing of God descends only upon those who work for God with love. (3)

Make room for God within yourself. This means making room for God within you. (5)

We have come to earth to learn to love God who has created us and loves us. When we learn how to love Him we shall understand the meaning of our life, and our relationships with others will become clear. (5)

There is One who loves you – that is God. Love God. Love Him who loves you. He has created you and loves you. Love Him as He is the first to have loved you. (5)

In the divine world, when you love someone you love everyone, and the opposite – when you do not love somebody, you love nobody. (4)

You should love God. If you do not love Him, you will understand neither Him nor those beings who were His helpers in creating the world. Your love of God is your eternal life. Hope, faith and love are the three stages in life. When you pass through them you will be able to work independently. (4)

Have faith and love God without expecting anything in return. Have boundless faith and selfless love. (4)

Do not expect anything from anyone. Be grateful for what God has given you. Rely on God. Be inwardly strong. Make way for the inner impulse within yourselves. It can unravel all entanglements. (64X)

Giving is one of the great processes of nature. The world gives one and takes two. God gives and does not take anything. (27X)

If you always think of God you will be blessed. No matter what you are doing, think of God. (7)

Try to please that God who lives within you, and who always sustains your mind, your heart, your spirit and your soul. (89X)

It is not important how people are considered by others, but rather what God thinks of them. (18X)

Our entire life has to be a constant effort to link ourselves to God, to be in constant contact with Divine Love, Divine Wisdom, Divine Truth, the Divine Spirit, the Divine Consciousness. These are living energies. Being in touch with them means feeling the bliss, happiness, power and rejuvenation which we desire. (50X)

Strive to attain the divine connection in your lives. When you achieve it, maintain it lest it be broken. You need to have an awakened consciousness if you want to keep it intact. (21X)

When you have that connection, every darkness will disappear from your mind and there will be no anxiety in your heart. There will be light in your mind, an expansive peace and joy in your heart; you will understand that God has visited you. (75X)

By our virtue we come to know God. As long as we are doing good, God is with us. The moment we sin, God leaves us and leaves us free to do whatever we like. When we sin we come to know God as mercy. He does not judge us but instructs us how to live. (7)

Remember: only God uses the law of freedom; He never uses violence. He works so deeply within us that we can never follow His path. Whoever works in this path and turns aside from it will pay a heavy price. (5)

If we do not accomplish the will of God, He does not blame us. He leaves us alone to do our own work. He only watches us and keeps quiet. If we do His will, He helps us in everything. (89X)

How am I to know the will of God? First of all, you
will have to study so as to know what it is and then fulfil
it. How shall I recognize it? You will sense a very
conscious inner achievement which has absolutely no need
of proof. (97X)

To serve God, to feel a connection with Him and always
to be ready to work for the divine cause – therein lies the
power, the wealth, the authority and the knowledge of
human beings. (78X)

The beauty of life lies in the fact that things do not
happen as we arrange them, but according to the will
of God. (56X)

You should offer your thanks only to God. God is the
primary source of all good. You should thank Him alone
and turn your mind and heart towards Him. (6)

The sublime law requires that gratitude and love for God
should always spring up within our hearts. (31X)

God created beauty. He created human wisdom, human
intelligence, human love and human power in order that
people should know His kindness. (3)

As soon as the thought comes to you to go to God,
approach Him with all possible humility. He is the only
One in the world who thinks at all times about all beings
from the smallest to the greatest. He foresees their needs
and satisfies them. He is love and acts towards all beings
with love. (3)

The path to God is a path of suffering. In this way you
will come to know Him. You will come to value what
God gives you, as well as what He takes away from you.
Suffering is the path to freedom. (4)

If the Lord does not use His hammer on some people, they
will remain ordinary stones without any value. (31X)

If you do not open your heart to God, you will be struck
by that karma which is your destiny. (8)

You may lose everything, but if you are in contact with
God you will resurrect and rise again. (5)

Always remember that there is something within you that is changeless - it is God within you who is changeless. (9)

Your bond with the great divine origin of life is a sacred thing. Nobody is permitted to cut this bond, and you have no right to cut it yourself. Rely on it: it will help you resolve the most complicated situations in your life. (9)

God responds to the prayer of every person, and gives something to everybody. When a bad person prays they will become good. When the sick pray, they will become healthy. If the good person does not pray they become bad. If the healthy do not pray, they become ill. (5)

When you encounter contradictions, inward struggle and doubt, turn to God within you and help will come immediately. (4)

God is infinitely patient and ready to forgive. (7)

Remember that God is active in every awakened soul. (4)

God is the centre around which you revolve. Everything revolves round this great divine centre. (4)

People have a mistaken understanding of God. They think that God is outside them in Heaven. Heaven is within you. (4)

Christ says: 'This is life eternal, to know Thee, the only true God.' To know God means to know ourselves, to know the primary principle which has sent us into the world; to know the unique One who loves us and who gives light, peace and joy to our souls. (6)

Rely on God within you. He will stimulate you to learn to work. (4)

The door of your mind and heart should always be open to hear the voice of God, who says: Emerge from your old understanding, from your old life and enter the new. (4)

Every person has a specific inner experience which enables them to recognize the divine voice within. (3)

To come to God means the disappearance of all that is negative within you, the vanishing of hatred, envy and suspicion. (10)

People cannot overcome their difficulties without coming into contact with God. (5)

If you come into contact with God even for a moment, all your misfortunes will melt away like ice. (10)

The power of human beings lies in doing the will of God. I say: God is within you. Give Him first place. Rejoice in God within you and leave Him free to work within you. God never limits your freedom. He expects you to open your heart to Him. (5)

The will of God is that you should understand the order of the divine world and live according to that order. When you live in this way, you will see that you are not far from the Kingdom of God. (3)

People who do not do the will of God are not humble. Why? Because the individualized part considers itself a centre round which everything must revolve and it is displeased that it cannot do what it wants. It says: I can use the good which God has given me for myself. That is not right for God; we will lose it. (6)

If you waver in fulfilling the will of God, you hinder your development. (3)

If you wish to appear before the face of God, be ready to do everything for Him. Therein lies the fulfilment of His will. (3)

Make room for God within you. Make room for every thought which comes from God no matter how small. It can always be realized. Never refuse to accomplish a thought of God. (5)

All people, all beings are parts of the divine organism. (39X)

One God, many friends. One God, many brothers and sisters. God is He who can unite us. (4)

God is coming into the world in a new way. He reveals Himself in all of us. He creates all anew. We shall be engineers of the new, builders of the new humanity. Through God who lives within us and through being conductors of His power, we can accomplish everything. (12)

To live in the Kingdom of God means to do the will of God. (4)

When you give the first place to God within you, then He will be able to help people and all living creatures. (13)

My task is to awaken that essential feeling for life and for God in human beings, so that they will believe in the good and sublime which is implanted within them. (27X)

People who do not love life do not love God either. (56X)

2

The Noetic World

The word noetic *and its cognates is used to denote the Bulgarian* razoumen, *meaning at once rational, wise and spiritually intelligent. The word also points to a deep inner meaning and relatedness subsisting between all things. The word is not simply a concept, but is experientially the light of God within corresponding to a particular level of being. The word noetic is derived from the Greek* nous, *meaning higher intelect, and contrasted with* dianoia, *signifying reason; the Latin equivalents are* intellectus *and* ratio. *Noetic knowledge and perception is unitive, leading to* noesis *or* gnosis, *while rational knowledge is dualistic and discursive, separating observer from observed, percipient from what is perceived; strictly speaking, only noetic perception leads to* episteme *or knowledge, while rational perception gives us* opinion. *The word* intellection *has become more or less redundant; and the word* intellectual *is loosely applied to an activity which is* rational. *Perennial philosophers such as René Guenon, Frithjof Schuon and S.H. Nasr have pointed out how rationalism and the so-called Enlightenment of the eighteenth century led to a systematic and categorical denial of any means of supersensible cognition by insisting that the only valid forms of knowledge were mediated by the senses.*

• • •

By the word *God*, which has lost its deep meaning in this epoch, we understand the noetic principle which created the world and which has provided all the conditions

necessary for the manifestation of life, and which directs
the whole of humanity and the whole of creation.
This great noetic principle penetrates and permeates
the whole of creation, operating within and outside it.
It also penetrates human beings. The meaning of light
in the physical world corresponds to that of the august
noetic principle for the whole cosmos, the whole
creation. (14)

By the word *God* we mean the noetic principle which
regulates and harmonizes physical, spiritual and divine
laws. (14)

The divine world is a world of perfection, a world of
harmony. (95X)

The divine world is the most beautiful world. People
cannot imagine such beauty. The beings who inhabit it are
beautiful, wise, intelligent and happy. There are no wiser,
more beautiful, more intelligent and happier beings. The
most enlightened beings are those who live in the divine
world. There is no other path for them than to enter this
world. There is no happiness outside this world. (3)

The divine life is distinguished by its unusual beauty and
majesty. There is nothing superfluous in the divine world.
Everything there is in its place. A traveller in heaven
would get lost among the beings there, because they all
resemble each other like one man. The only way of
recognizing your friend is through your love for him. (3)

Things are strictly determined in the divine world. There
is a definite time, place and means for everything. Things
do not happen mechanically there. When one person
eats, it is as if all are eating. There is no envy there. In
all the spheres of the spiritual world, what you buy in
the morning is all used up in the evening. If anything
is left over, try to distribute it immediately. There is no
insurance in the divine world. The earthly order differs
radically from the divine order. If you want to act
according to the laws of the divine world, all people must
be ready to understand its laws and live according to
them. (3)

If people only absorb divine knowledge themselves and do not pass it on to others, they are preparing the conditions of their death. One of the laws of the divine world is that 'People are obliged to share the goods they receive with others, having retained what they need for themselves.' (56X)

In the divine world it is the seed that is valuable. In the angelic world the blossom and stem are important; but in the human world it is the fruit. In the seed is hidden eternal life, immortality. (4)

The divine world has only one direction, only one point, one source from which all things proceed. This point is called *the eternal east*, the point of the eternally rising sun. (3)

Every noetic being is a conductor of divine energies. (15)

The noetic within easily resolves all difficult situations. It balances the forces of nature. (14)

In the noetic life there are no contradictions; a full harmony and unity reign. As soon as a person has balanced the influence of outside conditions and inner possibilities within himself, he enters the realm of the divine world, which then directs his life. Only under these circumstances does life acquire a full meaning. (17)

By the word *noetic* we mean those kinds of manifestation in which a person can see a consistent unbroken bond between all things in nature. Such a person can be called noetic because he sees the divine in operation through both good and evil. (6)

The noetic person is distinguished by the fact that he uses good and evil energies equally well. (46X)

Ideas are seeds which must be sown in order to grow up and bear fruit. The noetic principle requires you to plant your ideas in a good soil favourable to growth. The good person represents a fertile field, a ploughed soil in which you can sow divine ideas. Do not sow sacred divine ideas under unfavourable conditions. (3)

When love visits a person, he feels an inner expansion and is ready to serve himself, his household, society, nation, the whole of humanity and the noetic principle in the world – God. To serve the noetic principle means serving the whole. (14)

There is an inner law, a noetic consciousness which directs the consciousness of all beings. This essential consciousness directs all others and defines the position of each one in life. (6)

A person may have good conditions and possibilities at his disposal, but if his noetic faculty is not sound, he will not achieve anything. Good conditions and possibilities are raw material out of which nothing can be made. As soon as the noetic faculty or divine power comes to his aid, something valuable can be constructed from them. (14)

Noetic or right thought as a force is related to the divine world. The person who has it at his disposal is exempted from all contradictions in life. With the help of the noetic faculty he easily copes with every problem and builds up his life harmoniously. (14)

Therefore, since we are working with this living noetic force in the world, it will teach us how to live and act. (6)

All radiant and noetic beings manifest themselves through light and offer their services; all sublime and loving souls manifest themselves through warmth. (27X)

The angels relate to people through plants; they are their children. The archangels relate to people through mammals. Therefore people's attitude to plants and animals shows their human attitude to angels and archangels. (39X)

Every person is under special protection. Every human being is surrounded by noetic beings who stand guard. Nobody is alone in the world. People are surrounded by beings who are taking care of them. (26X)

Remember that it is not material wealth which gives meaning to life. People are striving towards an inner spiritual wealth. That is why they need to link themselves with the noetic world and with advanced beings. Real wealth is hidden within great souls. Nobody is able to advance without being linked to at least one great spirit. (58X)

Strictly speaking, music, poetry and art do not exist on earth. They are reflections of the divine world. So people can be musicians, poets, artists and scientists in so far as they are linked with the divine world. (86X)

Everybody should desire the coming of the Kingdom of God on earth! Everybody should desire that the will of God be done on earth! Everybody should stand on the side of wisdom and desire the coming of light and knowledge. Everybody should stand on the side of truth and wish to acquire freedom. This is the only way in which you will become transmitters of the divine and overcome all hardships. All of you are entrusted with missions to carry out. God has given you excellent bodies, radiant minds, noble hearts and strong wills; you have to retain these qualities. God has also given you a strong spirit and a great soul, in return for which you have to do His will willingly and with love. The person who realizes this has to say, 'We are going to work alongside all awakened souls – for the coming of the Kingdom of God on earth.' A challenge is issued throughout the world for all awakened souls to work in this way. (9X)

3

The Divine School, Master and Disciple

The Bulgarian word uchitel *means both teacher and master. The word* master *is more commonly associated with oriental gurus, but it does occur in the New Testament. As will be apparent from the introduction, Beinsa Douno was a Master in the full sense of the word. The word* uchenik *means both pupil and disciple (itself derived from the Latin word meaning to learn). The disciple is a kind of spiritual apprentice. I use the word here in preference to pupil, since it carries a spiritual connotation. It is, moreover, precisely defined by Beinsa Douno in relation to other stages on the spiritual path. The disciple is one who is consciously on the path to self-perfection.*

The essence of the divine school, formally opened by Beinsa Douno in 1922, was to give 'methods and rules for transforming the old into the new life', to integrate divine teaching into the practice of everyday living. The knowledge acquired is both practical, as can be seen from selections later in the book, and theoretical (in its true sense) from the Greek theoria, *the same root as theatre, meaning vision. The knowledge leads to understanding and wisdom, and can only be truly comprehended when it is applied to life and the gradual process of self-perfection and purification.*

The Master is a channel for, and a manifestation of, God, that is, an expression of Love, Wisdom, Truth, Beauty, Peace, Joy. The Supreme Master, though, is God 'who speaks inwardly to each soul, to each heart'. As Beinsa Douno puts it, 'The One who speaks down the centuries is always the same. At all times and in all places it is God who reveals Himself to humanity. The forms through which he manifests are different, but He is One.' The Master is pure, living as a divine exemplar, and can command the elements when necessary. Symbolically the Master is a source of living water and a sun of living light, a bearer of life, light and freedom: 'freedom for the soul, light for the mind, and purity for the heart'.

The disciple is the fourth stage of human development, the moment when the soul awakens to spiritual consciousness and begins to work for the good of the whole. The first category of persons are those of the Old Testament who simply work towards amassing wealth for themselves and are embittered by the mishaps of life. People of the New Testament look for sympathy and compassion; as soon as they find themselves suffering, or in difficulty, they become hesitant, succumbing to despair. The third category – the just – are looking for respect; they are saddened by setbacks and sensitive to any insults to their personal dignity. They want to be respected for themselves and appreciated for their actions.

It is only the disciple who does not seek wealth, sympathy, appreciation or respect. Disciples consider that difficulties are serious problems which need to be resolved, opportunities for learning about life. They do not criticize others and are not preoccupied by their faults. God is no longer the vengeful Jahweh of the Old Testament, but a God of Love, Light, Peace and Joy, which are also the qualities of the disciple. The disciple will be severely tested on the path and will have to make constant efforts to work on the gradual slope of spiritual ascent: 'The disciple will be subjected to tough trials in order to fortify his character and awaken his awareness. A life without trials is for slumbering souls.'

•   •   •

THE DIVINE SCHOOL

The divine school shows its disciples the right path by which to ascend the high divine summit which is the first to be illuminated by the divine rays of the rising sun. (17)

Every occult science belonging to the great science of life has as its goal the enlightenment of the human mind and the ennoblement of the heart as necessary conditions for correct human development. From this point of view, the mind and heart must help people towards rectifying their lives. (6)

The divine school prepares its disciples to be cornerstones of the noetic forces of nature. (13)

A prophet of the past expressed the idea of discipleship in a different way when he said: All people will acquire a new life, they will learn about God and will live in accordance with His requirements. This is true. A new life, a new work lies ahead of you. If you observe this great law – to read and study the great book of life, to study the life of the great people who have written it – it will give you valuable directions. The new science is formulating great methods and new ways of life for the future. Only the enlightened person who has resolved to serve God can see the future. A great future lies before you. (6)

The purpose of the divine school is to give methods and rules for transforming the old into the new life. (18)

The divine school is not designed to eliminate your sufferings but to show you how to extricate yourselves from them. (17)

The divine school recommends singing and playing musical instruments for the purpose of attunement and removing oneself from inharmonious and negative states. As long as we sing and play, our energies are positive and uplifting. (19)

The divine school gives the knowledge which enables you to correct your past. (17)

The significance of this life is the acquisition of knowledge. (15)

There is only a single sacred science in which many learned and consecrated people are working. They study the divine in life, and then open up their treasuries to display before the world their new knowledge and understanding. (6)

People need knowledge in order to set their thoughts
and feelings in order and to begin their spiritual
ascent. (27X)

Everyone possesses a certain amount of the new knowledge
which arrives at every moment. It is not enough simply to
keep this knowledge. One must be ready to receive the
new knowledge which is constantly arising, keeping up
with the new, because all things in life are subject to a
constant, uninterrupted progress. (14)

Knowledge without love makes people proud. Knowledge
with love gives significance to life and adorns it. (27X)

Some think that knowledge will come of itself and that
they will acquire knowledge without studying. That is a
false idea. People must observe, study, pore over things,
examining earth and heaven, the sun, the moon and the
stars, plants, minerals and animals, until they arrive at
positive and real knowledge. There are two kinds of
knowledge: the first is acquired by hard labour, and the
second by love. That knowledge which is acquired by love
is real. In such knowledge one sees the power deposited
within, the greatness of nature, the greatness of the
creator. The person who has attained that knowledge is
free from all criticism. (3)

The meaning lies not in knowing things but in
understanding them. (56X)

With the help of this new positive knowledge you will
build and improve your character so that you will be able
to overcome the difficulties lying in your path. (17)

A knowledgeable person is one who not only possesses
theoretical knowledge but who also masters the art of
living. (39X)

The talks given in the occult school must be studied in a
special way. Everyone should extract the most important
part of every talk and apply it in his life. (6)

People who have knowledge work to apply what
they know – in this way they gradually perfect
themselves. (46X)

Try to acquire something every moment, every hour, every day – no matter how small that something. If you work in this way, you will acquire much knowledge in a few years. (56X)

In every occult school there should form a general interest in the practical application of knowledge. (6)

Thus the divine teaching has an application to life and must be applied. If you have divine love within you, you will find people in this world with whom you will be in harmony and who will cooperate with you. But you must work for God. (6)

THE MASTER

When a Master comes to earth He does not speak from Himself or in His own name. He speaks in the name of HIM who has sent Him to earth. It is a pity when people do not benefit from the word of the Master. After 2000 years, this same Master will come and ask them: why did you not listen to the Master who spoke to you 2000 years ago? If you had obeyed Him you would not be suffering today. You listen but do not accept His words. (3)

The Master descends in order to manifest love. This is not an external process. The pure streams of love pass through Him towards all living things. Thus He wants to draw souls close to the light and joy in which He lives. (20)

The Masters bring sublime and radiant thoughts into the world by means of which humanity rises and advances. (27X)

The Master has four disciples in this world: Love, Light, Joy and Peace. If any of these disciples recommend you to Him, he will accept you into His school. If these four disciples credit you, the Master will open the doors of the school for you and give you free entrance, bless you and acquaint you with other disciples; from that moment you will be admitted to the school. (6)

When we speak of the Master we mean the great boundless
love that is expressed in giving knowledge, wisdom,
happiness and bliss to all living beings on earth.
That Being thinks of others every day. He thinks about
what shape He should give them. He hears the sighs of
the people, and all day long He thinks of how to improve
their existence. Such is the great Master: we all want to
give expression to His thoughts, His feelings and His
actions. (65X)

Every teacher at whatever level of development, or in
whatever world He may be, must give his disciples ways,
methods and elements with which to work. (6)

The requirement of a Master is that He should be able to
teach people how to build new spiritual dwellings in their
hearts and minds; He is a man who comprehends the
profound meaning of the elements that renovate their
bodies. (31X)

What makes the Master different? He is able to live in
both light and darkness, in hell and in paradise.
He is a Master of the laws of existence, which are at
His disposal. (27X)

The Master in the full meaning of the word has to be as
pure as crystalline water; He should be an example in
everything; He should have no hesitations, no ambiguity
or disbelief. (31X)

If you keep the sacred image of the Primordial Principle in
your minds you will be in touch with your Master – who
speaks to you from within every day and every hour. (39X)

The inner Master is whispering to us every minute, telling
us if we have acted well and if we have executed our tasks
properly. (26X)

There is a difference between the voice of the Master and
suggestion. Suggestion is a physical act which represents a
disturbance. When the Master is speaking, the disciple is
inspired. Freedom is always present in his discourse:
the disciple is free to accept or reject the Master's advice.
He does not force anybody. (39X)

When you approach your Master your health is restored, your heart is calmed and your mind becomes more radiant – He is really good, He is a Master, you think. So if you want to be a disciple, the first requirement is to have absolute faith in your Master. (13)

You cannot go alone to the Master. There must be a disciple to take you to Him. One disciple leads another disciple there. In the same way, there must be someone to lead us to God. (6)

There is a greater path than that of the disciple – that is the path of the Master. However, if you understand the path of the disciple you can come to understand the path of the Master. If you do not pass through the path of the disciple, the path of the Master will remain absolutely inaccessible to you. (6)

To be a Master, in the primary meaning of the word, is an act of higher self-consciousness, a pure spiritual process; both Master and disciple should be fully aware of the task they have to perform. There should be a complete exchange between them, as there is between mother and child: the Master has to state certain truths, while the disciple has to use them when needed. (31X)

THE DISCIPLE

You will recognize the disciple by the following qualities: he emanates a gentle light which does not cause any pain or hurt the eyes. He speaks with a gentle tone of voice which does not offend the ears. He feeds you with the kind of food which does not upset your stomach or taste. These things are not to be understood in a literal fashion, but by their inner meaning. When you experience a joy which banishes all contradictions you have scarcely experienced a fraction of the life of the disciple. This joy indicates a quality of the disciple. (6)

Disciples prepare the way for the coming of the Kingdom of God on earth. (6)

The way and path of the disciple must be the way of Love, Light, Peace and Joy. (6)

The disciple serves God consciously. (11)

Divine love gives a strong impulse to study divine wisdom. Study the principles lying behind all things. Everything you achieve in the present will be a help in the future. (11)

Obedience is the first quality of the disciple, who must be obedient to the noetic principle in nature. (13)

The disciple should live first for God, then for the soul, and then for the neighbour. (23)

The disciple should hold a high ideal towards achieving knowledge, freedom and love; nothing should be a distraction from this aspiration. (16)

It is very important for disciples to understand and correctly apply the laws of life. (6)

Disciples should possess not only theoretical but also practical knowledge of life. You should apply everything you learn in the school and make experiments yourselves. May the new teaching and the new life be embodied in you. (6)

Every disciple in the great school should work. Christ says, 'My Father works and I work.' Whoever does not work has no right to the goods of life. To work is to create. The disciple is not permitted not to work. (16)

I, who have realized that God has sent me to earth to do His will – I have to do as He desires. To be a disciple means consciously being a servant of God; that means knowing how to study. (107X)

The disciple should study occult science, but should not neglect official science which is the first step to the occult. Occult science is given by those advanced beings who guide the destiny of humanity. Official science is also valuable, but it confines its study to the outer side of life and nature. (13)

One thing is required from disciples: to understand their own moods and distinguish which are their own and which alien; also to discern their origin. Disciples should make an inner analysis and investigation of all their moods. (76X)

Love, Light, Peace and Joy are fruits of the Divine Spirit. These are the four subjects which the disciple begins to study at the outset of the path. (6)

As disciples of the occult school you should come to think exactly like a mathematician working with numbers and formulae. Every word you use should be a very clear expression of its meaning. (18)

The first requirement of a disciple is to make a space within for the inner truth. (18)

Disciples should learn to transform their desires. Every desire should be turned into a spiritual power. If you do not manage this, your life loses its meaning and becomes monotonous. It is our responsibility to give meaning to our lives and bring something new into them. The spiritual element within us makes, and gives meaning to, our lives. (16)

One of the fundamental qualities of the disciple is an ability to enter into contact with all beings and know that they are of value in the scheme of things. (13)

Fear is a great obstacle in the life of the disciple and should be eliminated. (25)

The disciple can overcome all obstacles! Disciples are characterized by a great humility and a great regard for all things. They always take last place, never think about themselves, but are at all times ready for complete self-denial. (6)

Some of you ask what distinguishes the occult disciple from an ordinary person? The difference lies in the fact that the occult disciple overcomes all difficulties in life. Truth is his ideal, wisdom his purpose, while love is his fulfilment. (25)

In the occult school there are difficulties which the disciple has to overcome so as to strengthen the will. When he comes to know the laws which regulate the inner and outer life, a great burden is removed and learning becomes much easier. (11)

The disciple should know that all actions are recorded in the memory of nature. (17)

The disciple should be awake at every moment to the possibility of doing something good. This means giving priority to the divine consciousness within. (13)

Obstacles in the path of the disciple are necessary for development. In overcoming the obstacles in life the disciple transforms negative forces into positive. (9)

The disciple should develop patience. (17)

Disciples of occult schools have always stumbled on account of their expectations. Disciples should not expect great results. All results are always microscopic. What you expect rarely happens. (68X)

When disciples are helped by the invisible world, all their affairs advance. If you have a desire to work, make the requisite efforts and the invisible world will assist you. (45X)

The disciple should keep promises. When a promise is given, it must be accomplished. To promise means to make a promise to the divine within you. It is permitted to postpone but not to change a promise. When the disciple does not keep a promise, inner peace is disturbed. (25)

Disciples should not be preoccupied with their own faults or those of others. When they study someone, they should seek out the good within him. The good lies deep within, and must be found. (28)

The occult disciple should have a well-developed intuition and should therefore work on it. Intuition is a considerable help in the life of the disciple; by means of it many misfortunes and troubles can be avoided. (6)

As disciples you must have a clear idea of the path of the disciple. We have nothing to do with people's mistakes and faults; they do not exist for us. We are concerned only with the one right life – the life of love. I say: God is a

God of Love, of Light, of Peace, of Joy. These are
therefore the qualities of the disciple. If you ask me what
your ideal should be in the present conditions of life,
I say that your ideal should be Love, Light, Peace and Joy
for all souls. This is not an ideal for eternity but one which
can be attained even today. (6)

First of all, as disciples of the occult school, you must
know how to guard the sacred knowledge you have
acquired and not display it on the market-place.
Knowledge is a fruit which ripens. Do not give this fruit to
anyone before you have tasted it yourself. (6)

Disciples should know in which world they are living – the
material, the spiritual or the divine. When they enter
the divine world their consciousness widens from that of
the caterpillar to the butterfly; that means, from the life
of limitations to the life of freedom. (26)

Disciples must have the forces hidden in the soul at their
disposal. They must foresee everything which may happen,
which is why they must always be on the alert with an
awakened consciousness. (6)

As disciples you should work on yourselves to get rid of
discontent. Make an effort but do not force yourselves.
People gain when making an effort but lose when they
force themselves. (3)

The task of the disciple is to expel all surplus thoughts and
feelings which might get in the way. (76X)

What is the most essential thing which disciples have
to ask their Master? They should say to Him: 'Master,
teach me how to walk straight along your path, to know
God as you know Him. Teach me to serve God as you
serve Him. Show me how to acquire the love you have for
God, for your own soul and for your neighbours.' (39X)

Christ says: 'The day is coming when those who hear my
voice will come out of their graves and will resurrect.'
Who will hear this voice? Only the disciples. Only they
will be renewed, only they will rise and be resurrected.
The new life, the resurrection, is only for them. It is

only for the disciples, for the people of the future, for the people of the new culture. They are the workmen in the Kingdom of God. They are the people of the new race; all people belonging to it will be of powerful mind, heart, soul and spirit. They will restore the Kingdom of God on earth and will say: it is possible for all of us to live in Love, Light, Peace and Joy, which God has given us. (6)

Twenty Rules Given by the Master to the Disciples

1. The path of the disciple is the path of the dawn. It is a path of eternal light that brings love.
2. The disciple should always have a straight posture which keeps the consciousness alert and produces a pleasant disposition to work.
3. Disciples always have the possibility of doing good. Doing good is the aim of their lives.
4. Disciples will be led into temptation so that their convictions will be tested.
5. The disciple has to put up with difficult trials so as to strengthen patience and alertness of consciousness. A life without trials is a life for sleeping souls.
6. The disciple should not be deceived by surface appearances and forms, but should search out the spirit of things.
7. The disciple prays alone. The prayer should be concentrated and its words taken to heart.
8. The disciple needs contemplation so as to get a sense of direction.
9. The disciple needs some seclusion so as to become inwardly strong.
10. There is nothing better for the disciple than purity. When disciples love, they should acquire purity. Love is a power that is unfolded only in purity.
11. When you are linked with God, you will experience no temptations.
12. Disciples of the occult school should never allow any doubt to creep into their minds with respect to divine providence. They know that the path they follow is a straight one.

13. Doubt is an issue for the disciple, one which must be properly resolved.

14. The law of love decrees that as soon as you begin to love, everything becomes radiant for you. Thus you will understand that you are in the field of love, where there is no doubt. There is no doubt within love.

15. The first test of the disciple is the test of doubt. That is why you have to spend a night of doubt and overcome it alone.

16. The disciple has to pass through doubt. It is a region which has to be crossed to its very end. Disciples will find themselves in a northern polar night – a night that lasts six months, but they have to understand the law. The night has to be endured and they must stand firm the whole time. When that period of darkness and inner eclipse has passed away, enlightenment will come; the radiant day and the consecration will come as well.

17. The disciple should see something good everywhere and in everyone. People who see crimes, vices and shortcomings everywhere have a leprosy in their heart; it is dreadful to have the devil in your heart.

18. As long as disciples are tempted by the world, you cannot tell them anything about God. Some darkness should fall from the outside, so that some light can spring up in the soul. The love of Christ is born only when there is some inner light. Disciples should not rely on the light of the world. They should heed and guard the light within their souls.

19. The disciple cannot at the same time be friends with the world and with God. If the disciple loves God, the world will become dark; it will fade away and disappear. Meanwhile, the disciple will be in another world – a world of Light, Peace and Joy; there the words of the Master will be heard.

20. The path of the disciple is a pleasant one in spite of all its hardships, because it is a path of ascent. (21)

4

Fundamental Principles of Life

The kernel of Beinsa Douno's teaching lies in the principles of Love, Wisdom and Truth:

God is Love, Wisdom and Truth. Christ is the manifestation of God.

Christ is divine love, divine wisdom, divine truth, which must be lived and applied by all men and women.

We preach the Christ of love, which supports and fills all hearts;

We preach the Christ of wisdom, which illuminates every mind;

We preach the Christ of truth, which liberates and elevates the world.

Love excludes hatred, violence, murder.

Wisdom excludes ignorance, error, darkness.

Truth excludes lies, slavery, sin.

There is nothing greater than these three principles; there is no surer and straighter path. In these three principles lies the salvation of the world.

Expressed in terms of a formula:

> Love brings Life
> Wisdom brings Light
> Truth brings Freedom.

As in Christian teaching, the essence is love. Beinsa Douno distinguishes four levels of the manifestation of love: aspiration in the heart, feeling in the soul, force in the mind and principle in the spirit. In Beinsa Douno's metaphysics, heart corresponds with soul, and mind with spirit, as the four levels of the human being. The expression of love moves from the exclusive towards the inclusive, from the circle of two individuals to the all-embracing circle of divine love; the first two levels of love are physical, the last two divine.

More specifically, love as aspiration in the heart, corresponding to the roots of the tree, is the stirring of emotional love. Love as feeling in the soul, corresponding to the branches, reaches up towards God and is expressed in brotherly and sisterly friendship. Love as a force in the mind, corresponding to the blossoms or flowers, is an evolved form of love found in those who are prepared to live for and defend the divine cause. Saints and geniuses such as Schweitzer and Gandhi have understood truth and lived it out, making whatever sacrifices are necessary. Love as a force resonates powerfully as an inspiration through human culture. No one has had such an impact in this respect as Christ himself. Finally, love as a principle in the spirit, corresponding to the fruit, is a supreme and all-encompassing harmony which has scarcely made an appearance in the world.

This can be summed up schematically:

Aspiration in the heart	*Roots*	*Personal emotion*
Feeling in the soul	*Branches*	*Brotherly/sisterly concern*
Force in the mind	*Flowers*	*Manifestation of divine qualities*
Principle in the spirit	*Fruit*	*Supreme harmony*

LOVE

Love is a principle which cannot be explained theoretically, as a result of which it is not understood. (3)

Love is the essence of life. (29)

Love gives life to human beings. (90X)

Love is the medium in which we humans exist and without which we cannot exist. (76X)

Love is a special cosmic energy that passes through all living beings. (7)

The cohesion of matter depends exclusively on the love existing between its particles and which makes them attract each other. (108X)

Love is the first and last door through which we enter. Every other love is nothing but a reflection of a small light and does not resolve any of the problems of life. The only love which resolves all life's problems is divine love. The other kinds are also valuable, but they will be in their place only when the love of God remains in the centre of human life. (3)

Where love is, there life is. When love is absent, life vanishes. The coming of love means the resurrection of the soul. The person who attains love resurrects, while the person who loses love dies. (3)

Therefore we cannot have in our life any other foundation than love. And we cannot acquire love until we begin to love God. First of all we must love God. If we do not love God we cannot love men. (6)

Human love is partial, while the love of God is complete and whole. By the term *whole* is meant an integrity, a unity of all kinds of consciousness. If you love all people, their consciousness will unite with yours after they receive your love. Thus a unity of consciousness will be achieved. (6)

Love includes the good of all beings. (30)

Love always considers the good of others, not its own good. (30)

To love your neighbour means to give them inwardly all the rights you would wish for yourselves. (9)

Try to love all people as souls. Discover the great and beautiful in people like the jeweller distinguishes precious stones from ordinary ones and sells them expensively. The slightest light in a person's soul is a precious stone. Find that stone, put it in its proper place and give it the requisite value. This means raising a person up. (27X)

To love a person means to act in such a way as never to force them. How do we understand this? Never eat the bread they eat; never drink the water they drink; never covet the house where they live; never envy their clothes, shoes or hats; never cross the path which is theirs; never take their seat. This is the meaning of love. (9)

When you love somebody you need to remember never to misuse their goodness. (58X)

People should observe and study the phases of love: animal love, human love, angelic love, finally coming to divine love. As long as people are only interested in material life, they remain within the bounds of the animal world; when they are interested in material and spiritual life, they are within the bounds of human love; when the passions disappear from human life, they reach angelic love. And finally, if people understand the causes underlying the phenomena of life, they enter into divine love. (29X)

There is no being more beautiful, more powerful and more noble than love. (6)

There is nothing more beautiful than an encounter between two souls who love each other. (76X)

When two people love each other, light flows from one to the other. If there is no light flowing in and out of them, they do not love each other. (76X)

Love is the eldest sister, the highest daughter of God born in eternity. Light is the eldest brother, also born in eternity. Peace is the most beautiful home that joy can inhabit. In the future, if you want to build your bodily home, peace must assist you. Such is the law. And then joy will come and live in this body. If you have no peace, joy can never come to earth. (6)

The real, the true measure is the sublime love that has nothing whatsoever to do with ordinary human feelings and moods. The quality of such love is known by the fact that its coming into contact with a stupid person makes them clever and wise; when it touches the dead, it brings them back to life and resurrects them; when it touches the leper, his leprosy disappears forthwith; when it touches the disheartened person it gives them courage. Sublime love works wonders. Wherever it goes, it creates and reconstructs. We need to study such love. (64X)

Why did Christ come to earth? What was his task? To apply the law of living love which solves all problems – mental, emotional and social ones. When you apply living love, you will see that all people feel like you. They rejoice and suffer like you. They all have the same needs as you. When you comprehend that, you will be able to feel sympathetically disposed towards everybody – then you will be able to help them as you help yourself. (64X)

The essential qualities of love are that it bestows freedom and sacrifices everything. (29X)

You should love as God loves. He loves people for what they are, not for their riches, their power, knowledge, beauty or virtue. (26X)

The strongest feature of love on the physical plane is movement. Wherever there is movement, there is great love. The most powerful feature of love in the astral world is feeling; in the mental world it is thoughts and the process of thinking; in the causal world, the root causes. The love of the person who lives in the causal world is strong and unchangeable. We may apply the following proverb to such a person: 'A word given is a stone thrown.' (81X)

Love is the only eternal element. It is boundless. All other things outside love are transitory. (40X)

Wisdom is a method of God's love – and is therefore also included within love. Truth is a seed, also included in love. What then is justice? It is also included in love. If, then, you manifest love, all virtues will be manifested. (40X)

There is only one path in love: the path of wisdom. Love brings one gift: virtue. Love makes use of only one right: divine justice. (64X)

Love contains a mighty power. It works wonders. People are prepared to do you favours on account of their love. They would never do so otherwise. (27X)

It is only love that is able to break the chains of evil. (90X)

One day love will stand above everything. It will wipe out all defects. It is the only power that sets everything to rights. Leave everything to love. It will put everything right. (38X)

When the love of God penetrates people, they experience a warm expansive feeling towards everything alive in the world. They are not petty. They see everything properly. Nothing is able to make them angry. They know that the warm feeling they have in their hearts is worth more than any riches in the world. (121X)

Under the influence of love, human conceptions are formed and transformed. These changes are similar to the alterations endured by amber before it turns into a diamond. You should think of love as a power and a principle until you reach its positive meaning. (81X)

Love is a tender bloom that grows and unfolds away from the public gaze. Nobody should know anything about your love. (81X)

Love contains light, warmth, thoughts and conditions for growth, blossoming and bearing fruit. (18)

The greatest art of all is the art of loving. (67X)

There is a single law in the world: the law of love. (64X)

We are going to raise our consciousness to universal love. You will feel the vibrations of all suffering people and you will hear their voices – this will mean that you will be able to help yourself, your people and humanity at the same time. The person within whose heart that feeling has awakened and is active – the person who has freed himself from all material handicaps – will be able to project everywhere in space and help everyone. (4X)

I should like every thought or feeling or action – whatever it is – either in the physical, spiritual or mental world, to be performed with love, to be permeated with love. (65X)

Remember: you cannot live well if you have no faith and hope. These are the two hands of love. Do not separate faith from love. Do not separate hope from love. Faith is the hand which helps the mind, and hope the hand which helps the heart. (4)

Love is the divine source of life. Through love we enter on the right path of life, where there is no death. When we enter on the path of wisdom we emerge from the darkness which is the cause of great suffering in our lives. We have to thank God for joys and sufferings which ultimately bring the great benefits of life. (5)

If you have known divine love, human love has no significance. The love of God gives meaning and value to human love. Only in this way can human love be harmonized with the divine. (4)

There is something more real than riches, namely being in contact with the love of God within yourself. This is the most important reality. When you attain this love, all contradictions disappear. If you wish to understand this great love in the right way, listen to the still voice within you. (5)

The purer and more sublime your love becomes, the greater the possibility of knowing the One who loves you. He will gradually reveal Himself to you, and you will begin to see inside and outside equally clearly. (3)

Love is a great stimulus in life. We all need an inner impulse, an inner stimulus to push us forward. There is no progress without this stimulus. Love is this stimulus. You cannot make any progress without love. You must love at least one noetic being, on whose account you will study. You must not live only for yourselves, but for others also. To live for others is to give an impulse to the divine love within you. If, therefore, you love God, He will be an inner stimulus within you and you will be able to manifest your soul. (6)

If I am by a mountain spring and a man asks me for a cup of water, should I fear that if I give him a cup of water there will be no water for tomorrow? The spring flows constantly – it has conviction. The springs of the divine world never become dry. Suppose that love enters a person and begins to spring forth. However, that love diminishes daily until it stops flowing. After some time it starts flowing again. Does this love move along the way of conviction? No, for there is an interruption in it. So when there are interruptions in love it is temporary and human, not eternal and divine. (3)

If you want people to love you, you have to be like fruits. If you want the angels to love you, you should become like light. If you want to love, you have to come to God. Only in this way can you love all people. (4)

The first manifestation of love is giving. Give purely and uncovetously. The person who does not give cannot love. (3)

God manifests Himself in the physical world through giving. So be generous like God. (50X)

Every body that gives out light is called shining and bright. Bodies that receive the light, absorbing it within themselves, are called dark. Radiant personalities are those people who are constantly sending out light, that is, who are constantly giving. (57X)

The divine order requires us to give. The person who gives is good. They are good as long as they give, but as soon as they stop giving they cease to be good. The good person does not retain anything for himself. Since such a person does not retain anything within himself he does the will of God and therefore enjoys an inner peace.(3)

Life gives and death takes away. Giving is an inner but not an outer process. God participates in giving. It is said that God is love. That means that when love comes it attracts life, and life attracts all forces and energies in nature. (4)

The act of giving is related to the external side of love, while conviction is linked to the internal side. The power of conviction can be seen in its application. If a certain conviction cannot be applied in the physical world it cannot be applied in the spiritual world either. The divine teaching can be applied in all worlds. We simply have to know how to apply it. The difference lies only in the way

of application, not in the fact that it is possible or
impossible to apply. (3)

Everyone speaks about love. How do you know that a
person has love? Where there is love, there is always
giving. It is impossible for a person to have love and not
to give. When love leaves a person, they stop giving. Love
expands people and arouses in them the desire to give.
This law can be tested everywhere in life. Give as long as
you have love within you. Giving is an inner process
which unites people with God. The person who does not
give cannot be in contact with God. (3)

The person who desires the love of others but does not
give of himself cannot be loved. Let such a person first
give of his love and it will be given to him. Unless you
first give your heart, you will remain far from love. (3)

Therefore be pure, saintly, powerful and full of love if you
want people to love you. Today all people are candidates
for love, that is, all wish to be loved, but they must know
that only what is perfect can be truly loved. (3)

I am not referring to human love which enslaves people.
It is like love of wine. It enslaves and annihilates. Such a
love makes a person go down and to the left. Now I advise
you to accept the love which leads you upwards and to the
right. This is the love of the eternal light and eternal life. It
brings with it new knowledge. I wish you to enter the
world of divine love and say: Let us be done with the old
world and the old conception of life. We enter the new
life, the life of new conceptions which bring new freedom.
In this way a person will be freed from his weaknesses and
enter the world of eternal bliss. This means that divine
consciousness penetrates human consciousness. Then the
person becomes one with God. This is why we have come
to earth. Liberation does not come from weeping despair,
but through hard work in one direction. That means work
on the mind, the heart and the body. The time has come
for single-minded conscious work. The contradictions of
life should be banished. Thus you will come to tread the
path which leads to eternal love and which brings all
abundance of life. (4)

As people do not understand love, they encounter sufferings. There are three agents which cause people suffering: hunger, fear and human love. Hunger induces people to commit many crimes. Fear is the root of many great evils in life. People speak theoretically and abstractly about love. They speak about divine love without any understanding. They speak about human love, but do not understand that either. It is not enough for a person to love; that love must also bear fruit. If it does not bear fruit, love cannot be understood. (3)

When we speak about love we mean that unique power which can accompany you throughout your difficult path and lead you safely out. It is the only human comfort in the heavy and difficult hours of life. This is what it means to be carried in someone's arms. Only love can carry you in its arms. (6)

Today the need is for strong souls, strong disciples who will not only speak about love but also manifest and apply it in life so that they may support and uplift those suffering souls. (6)

When you love you are born; when you hate you die.
Until you leave life, you live; when you come to darkness you die.
The good one is born, the bad dies.
This means that the positive brings light and the negative death. (4)

There is no power in hatred. The power lies in love.
Ignorance does not bring strength. Strength lies in knowledge.
Power is in the good, not in the evil. (4)

Thus you must start with love. Love must be born within you. In order for it to come to birth, there must be a material form through which it can be manifest. (6)

In order to acquire knowledge and profit from your life experience, you must pass through the portals of love. (3)

May love come and kindle that sacred fire within you. That means God coming to live in all people. Then the Kingdom of Heaven will come on earth. All men and women will come to know God. (4)

WISDOM

Divine wisdom is a basic principle that supports life. (32)

Wisdom carries divine light and divine knowledge. They create beauty and order in life. (33)

It is wisdom that will save the world. (27–212)

Wisdom is the link with the minds of all noetic beings. (105X–13)

There is a divine philosophy. A divine wisdom in the world, which has existed from time immemorial. (27–340)

Divine wisdom is the principle that can bring some light and knowledge into human minds. Wisdom makes people wise and shows them the right manner of living. (64X–29)

Wisdom contains divine light and divine knowledge, which create beauty, law and order in life. (14–112)

When someone speaks of divine wisdom, I understand it to mean all the light in limitless space – the light that never fades. (105X–19)

When people enter into contact with the law of wisdom, light will begin to flow from their minds. Then no one will stumble: their path will be flooded with light. (72X–17)

Divine wisdom is a basic principle that supports life. Without the wisdom within life, it would have been annihilated long ago. (22–19)

When you devote your lives to wisdom, you will understand that you have knowledge and light to see things clearly. (23–8)

Who is wise? The person who does not make mistakes. (93X–149)

Christ said: 'I am the Way, the Truth and the Life.' The way is that of knowledge, the boundless divine wisdom which you need to study. (89X–199)

Saint Paul also wishes to show that the love of wisdom is the path to salvation. (47–11)

Wisdom represents the most difficult path in life. There is no path more difficult than the path of wisdom. (105–13)

Without study, you will never acquire either wisdom or knowledge. (97X–142)

The sublime thoughts originating in wisdom bring light into human minds. (27–5)

I do not believe that there is a single one among you that does not desire to have wisdom in their mind. (63X–189)

The person who has joined wisdom with love has become truly alive. (61X–76)

You are a real human being as long as you hold firmly to the principles of love and wisdom. Outside these principles people do not exist as noetic and conscious souls. (27–183)

If a person has love as a basis and the two pillars of wisdom and truth as a support, they will be able to cross the vast ocean of life safely from coast to coast. (71X–121)

Wisdom represents the external, the tangible, the visible form of things; love is the content of these shapes, while truth is their meaning. (81X–92)

It is wisdom that brings fulfilment to the spirit. (101X–88)

Be a spring of light and wisdom! (111X–59)

TRUTH

Truth is eternal light, eternal wisdom, eternal love, eternal justice and eternal life. (3X)

Truth is a higher manifestation of love. Truth is the purest image of love. It is eternal life. (3X)

Whatever throws light on love is truth. (105X)

Only the radiant path of wisdom leads to truth. Life is hidden in truth. (113X)

The light you have has come from the light of truth. (13X)

People must live in the conviction of truth; such people neither waver nor faint. (6)

Wherever disputes predominate, truth can never appear.
Truth grows and unfolds in peace and calmness. It grows
in peace and love. (30)

When you come to know the truth, you will experience a
deep inner peace. (4)

What does truth represent? It is a special state of the
human soul which is in a state of total peace and harmony
with the source of life. It is truth which determines
human attitudes towards the supreme principle of
life. (64X)

The person who speaks the truth will taste all the blessings
of life. He who does not speak the truth will experience all
the sufferings of life. If you do not want to suffer, be
always on the side of truth. What are the rules of truth?
These rules are inscribed in your heart. Open the book of
your heart and read. (3)

Truth leads to resurrection. Lies end in death, the truth in
life. (3)

Whoever has the truth within himself has strength.
Whoever has goodness within himself always has life.
Hold to truth and goodness. Thus you have life and
strength. (36)

Truth is a transformer. It helps you overcome your
difficulties. Truth helps you resolve your contradictions.
Truth gives the true value of things. It reveals their
reality. (7)

To acquire truth is to have inner knowledge, an inner
understanding of things. (32)

Initiation is connected with truth. Whoever has truth
within himself is an initiate. Where there is true initiation
there are no contradictions, no death. But in order to come
to that initiation one has to suffer. (4)

When they asked Jesus why he had come to earth, why he
had been born, he said: 'To this end have I come into the
world: to bear witness of the truth. Everyone who is of the
truth hears my voice.' I say that the path of every man

who has come to bear witness of the truth is tragic and dramatic. It is full of tragedies and dramas. The path of every seeker of the truth is paved with dramas and tragedies. And if you ask me now why you must suffer, why you must be unfortunate or die, I will say to you: this is necessary so that you may pave the way of truth. You will be the living stones which will pave the way where truth will pass. (6)

If you cannot serve the truth and the good you have understood nothing. These are two essential things. What is good? It is the basis of life. What is truth? It brings freedom. (5)

The Spirit of God, truth, which is within you, will make you free. (39X)

Freedom is an inner process. It is a contact with the thought of God. Only the person whose thought is connected with the thought of God is free. (6)

The person with light in their mind, heart and will is free. (4)

Freedom must be given to everyone so that they may manifest themselves according to their level of consciousness. Do not exert violence on human consciousness. Everyone must act freely. (3)

Truth is one. We cannot therefore speak of an old and a new truth. The truth is one, unchangeable and essential to every human life. (64X)

People should realize that God has placed the truth within them. Truth lies in the fact that people begin to realize that God is living within them and they are living within God. (55X)

As long as you are empty and the truth is not within you - be quiet, do not speak, let your bottle be filled. As soon as the truth enters you and fills you - begin to speak, tell the truth to everybody, so that your bottle will empty itself and begin to fill up again. (25X)

The first thing to love is the truth. The best and most

beautiful thing is to speak the truth. There should be absolutely no lies! (109X)

Only those souls who love one another are living in the truth. (64X)

Here is a way of understanding the truth: 'Every tree is known by its fruits. Wait until it bears fruit.' (107X)

Truth is what we plant, and the fruit of which we taste. Light enables truth to manifest. (68X)

FREEDOM

If you look at a person with the eyes of a clairvoyant you will see the following picture: many threads emanate from the person and these threads tie him down. The threads are like the rays of the sun. As long as a person is tied by these threads, he always feels hampered: he wishes to think, but cannot manage it; he wishes to feel, but cannot manage this either; he wishes to display his will freely, but again this is impossible. He wants to tear these threads, but is unable to do so, ignorant as he is of the laws of breaking free. To be free, you need to pray, to make an effort, you need to tear these threads carefully until, one day, you begin to feel your thoughts liberated, your feelings set free, your actions freely chosen. (28–148)

All of you are faced with the solving of a most important problem: that of being a slave or being free; the service of necessity or the service of freedom. The word freedom means awakening, serving the spirit. (28–148)

Freedom means the most sublime quality within people. (109X–45)

The aspiration and the striving of the human soul is towards freedom. That is a great inner impulse of the conscious person, not of ordinary people. It is an inner stimulus in people as, and when, the divine awakens within them. (115X–44)

Freedom is an aspiration of the human mind, heart, soul and spirit; freedom is life. (31–105)

Freedom means a noetic limitation. No matter how free a person is, they cannot step outside the laws of nature. (71X–3)

To improve people's fate does not mean being completely liberated from their burden, but learning how to bear it and which path to tread. (7–50)

A wide scope of action is the distinguishing feature of freedom. (31–109)

Freedom is linked with knowledge. The person with knowledge is the only one who can be free. (46–33)

Without knowledge of the truth, freedom is impossible. (38–4)

God has given us full freedom in the world and tells us: 'I give you life, and you can dispose of it as you please.' (14–136)

I should like to lead you to an inner contact with the great living laws through which God rules the world. Those laws make people absolutely free to do what they like, but through these laws they are held responsible for their actions. (83X–6)

Whether we are kings or simple folk, the spirit within us wants to be free. (31–96)

Freedom is essential for the growth of that high ideal towards which humans strive. (109X–47)

When you work upon yourself, you will become a free person. (96X–27)

How can people attain freedom? Through conscious work upon themselves. They have to possess a measure of love, wisdom and truth. (72X–31)

A free person is one with an excellent mind, an excellent heart, an excellent will, an excellent soul and an excellent spirit. Freedom results from hard work upon oneself. (87X–35)

People can have a conscious or unconscious attitude towards the beings above them: this attitude determines their own freedom. (21–301)

The only person who is free is one who has found the truth. (116X–13)

Until a person has brought mind, heart and will into balance and in accordance with truth, he cannot he free. (27–108)

When we say: Truth will make us free, it means that only the sublime noetic element in the world will make us free. (112X–49)

The person who lives in that sacred unchanging world where God lives, and who listens to God, understanding His laws and instructions – only such a person is free and able to exercise the will freely. (31–134)

We will be free when we accept God within ourselves and within our hearts. (117X–49)

People should do only what arises from within in accordance with the spirit and with the disposition of the mind and heart. Only thus will they feel themselves as souls free from every limitation and external influence. (118X–120)

If you are rich and strong, you can be free only physically. (109X–56)

People are free only when they think. (45–3)

There are countless beings imprisoned and awaiting liberation. Why? Because they wish to go in all directions, while freedom means moving in only one direction. (109X–45)

As soon as you desire something you are locked up. As soon as you throw away one desire, you are free. There are certain desires which should not be attained. (119X–53)

You are able to be free when realizing one of your desires only when your mind has taken part in forming the desire. (46–33)

People begin to work consciously when freedom comes. (26–181)

When people give freedom to others, they abolish their karma. (23)

If you want freedom for yourselves, you have to give freedom to others as well. (31-51)

This is the creed of Christ that I am preaching - to have and to give freedom, to have and to give freedom, and again to have and to give freedom: every kind of freedom - mental, emotional, religious, civil and domestic freedom. Freedom everywhere. (31-96)

● ● ●

LOVE, WISDOM AND TRUTH

Love is the heart of God, wisdom the head of His word and truth His feet. The person who loves God has balanced the energies of their heart and is ready to sacrifice everything for God. (3)

Love gives, wisdom contains, truth distributes. (3)

By wisdom we understand the manifestation of love and truth. (3)

Wisdom gives the form of things, love the content and truth the meaning. (17)

Wisdom represents the external, the real and visible form of things, love the content of those shapes, while truth is their meaning. (3)

Truth joined to virtue is righteousness. (38)

Wherever righteousness and justice reign - there is law and order, there is freedom. As regards freedom, it is the external side of justice. (39)

In the good everything grows and lives. Everything rises and acquires life. (4)

The person who has love is strong. You can all have this power, as it is obtained by grace, without any violence. As far as wisdom, truth, knowledge and the rest of the virtues are concerned, you pay for them with your blood. The only virtue given freely is love. (6)

Love the perfect way of truth and life.
Place good as the foundation of your home,
Righteousness as a measure of your life,
Love as an adornment,
Wisdom as the defending wall
And truth as the light of your path.
Only then will you come to know me,
And I shall reveal myself to you. (40)

5

Divine and Natural Laws

With our western scientific culture, we know more about natural than divine laws. Indeed, many people are sceptical of the very existence of divine or spiritual laws. By law, in this context, is meant the structures governing our inner life, rather than decrees or commandments. Such laws are discovered through the trial and error of experience, and lead to insight and wisdom. The inner law of love, of giving, is a way of accomplishing the divine will; infringements bring suffering which, in turn, produces insight. The following quotation illustrates the point:

> Purely human love leads to
> suffering,
> Suffering gives experience,
> Experience engenders knowledge,
> Knowledge brings wisdom,
> Wisdom leads to Truth.

and the rationale:

> Human love changes and varies,
> Spiritual love varies without changing,
> Divine love neither changes nor varies.
> It simply grows.

One of the fundamental strands running through the quotations which follow is that of reciprocity, exchange and *proportion in terms of giving and receiving, sowing and reaping. Life always seeks balance through alternating polarities. Thus we are encouraged to learn the law of the transformation of energy through joys and sufferings which inspire and impel us forwards. All the inner laws given below can naturally be tested against our own understanding of life as we progress along the path of self-development. They serve as reflections which give a perspective on our affairs.*

• • •

The world in which we live is ruled by laws and regulations established by God aeons ago when He was forming the universe. If you observe the divine laws you will always be happy, joyful and blessed; you will succeed in all your undertakings. (38)

The laws are the results of truth. (7)

The laws which God has created must be studied because, personal or individual, mental and spiritual life is based upon them. (6)

Divine laws admit no exceptions. (3)

The divine always conquers, while the human is always conquered. This law is without exception. (25)

In order to be able to distinguish the divine from the human and animal, you have to learn the law of differentiation and overcome your weaknesses. Your weaknesses are due to the influence of base beings which are like parasites. You must keep away from these dangerous influences. That means having inward vision. (26)

The disciple should know that things are better accomplished in silence than when speaking about them. According to occult laws you may speak about something after you have finished it. You must recognize conditions you meet as problems to be solved. (25)

Your karma can be abolished through the law of love. (9)

Divine knowledge is acquired and developed only through the law of love. (6)

The only success which will be harvested in the world is through love, including knowledge, wisdom, the divine life, justice, conscience, righteousness, the virtues, etc. Everything high and noble has a great future. So every one of your acts born of love will succeed. Every thought, every desire born of love, no matter how small it may be, will succeed. (6)

Live therefore according to the inner law of love, the law of giving. In this way you will test whether you have love or not. (3)

I give the following rule to the disciple – if somebody asks you for something, do not be in a hurry to give it to them straight away. Do not give anything unless you have that inner impulse of love: to give. (83X)

The divine law states: freely you have received, freely give. In other words: you must give everything that is given to you. The person who is not ready to sacrifice everything for the divine cannot attain anything. (3)

One of the laws of the divine world is: people are obliged to share the goods they receive with others after they have retained what they need for themselves. (41)

If you give much, you will receive much. If you give little, you will receive little. If you sow much, much you will reap. If you sow little, you will reap little. That is the law. (42)

There is a law: if you give, it will be given to you in turn. This is called the law of universal abundance. (6)

It is a law: the sublime invisible world helps only the good and the wise. If you want their help, you should help others. (43)

There is a law which states that if you pay heed to the freedom of other people, they will respect your freedom. People will act towards you as you do towards them. You should have regard for the smaller beings: 'With what measure you mete, the same shall be meted unto you.' If you measure with the law of love, wisdom and truth, it will be meted out to you with the same measure. (14)

In order to live well, people need to study not only the laws of outer pressure and inner tension, but also those of time with which the noetic world operates. For every good which is given to us, there is a definite time assigned. The same law applies to good fortune. (14)

If people do not want to suffer, they must respect the law of exchange, which states that one receives as much as one has given. (14)

Many people think that if they live alone, away from others, they will progress faster. To think in this way is to fool yourself. Once one comes to earth among people, animals, plants and minerals, one cannot be free from their influence. Even the smallest particle which surrounds a person exercises an influence but they, in turn, also influence all living beings. The whole of nature influences human beings, but they also influence nature. This law is unavoidable. (3)

The law of mutual aid states that there can be no connection between people unless they are permeated by a strong desire to help each other. (45)

There is a divine law which satisfies every need of life. Every divine need is satisfied in time, but you must first have the desire to accomplish the will of God. First do the will of God, then your own. (5)

If you do the will of God, you give one and gain ten. If you do your own will, you give one and lose ten. There is no exception to this law. (4)

You must have a clear idea about the inner motives which underlie the outer motives of contemporary people. It is not enough to know about human motives; you should also know those of the whole organic kingdom. This law, this reality in life is a noètic one, but all beings do not have the same degree of perception. (6)

Beautiful and great things come into being during difficult periods in life. Such is the law. The greater the difficulties, the greater the good which is contained within them. (27)

Through sufferings and joys one learns the law of the transformation of energy. (43)

You need to learn the law of economizing your energy, in order to do a great deal of work with little energy. (43)

There is an inner law by which faults get piled onto the back of the person who wants to correct those of other people. (6)

The interests of the parts cannot be reconciled among themselves. They can be reconciled only within the whole. The *whole* represents a great law for the reconciliation of the parts. Therefore, anyone who has dealings with the parts must first of all understand the law of the whole, since every part has its definite place within the whole; it is a part as long as it maintains its own place. If it loses its place it ceases to be a part. The same theory can be observed in life. (6)

Only the whole is free. Thus, whenever we want to give freedom to the parts, the whole becomes limited. (6)

All these laws can be applied when we enter the divine teaching. This is why all are required to learn. (6)

6

The Human Being

No more fundamental question can be asked than this: What is the nature of a human being? Answers to this question fall into two basic categories: the orthodox scientific approach sees the world and humanity as an outcome of blind chance, the universe as an accident – one of those things that happens from time to time. The corollary of this view is that human consciousness is a by-product of the brain which perishes at bodily death. The true view, however, is based on traditional religious and spiritual beliefs which set chance within a world of purpose and propose that human beings are more than physical bodies. They say more – the essential self transcends the death of the body.

Beinsa Douno's metaphysics sees four basic principles in the human being, namely, heart, mind, soul and spirit; etymologically, the soul is the animating principle (anima in Latin) while the spirit is the breath (pneuma in Greek, spiritus in Latin). So long as the animating principle of life and breath is expressed in the human body, we remain alive on earth. When it withdraws, we experience physical death. In Beinsa Douno's philosophy, the human soul is originally a divine ray emitted by God in whom souls eternally live and move. Although souls have an underlying unified existence, they are all different in that 'each soul represents a state of divine consciousness'. Divine consciousness manifests in souls as different states in space-time. Beyond and behind this separation, though, all souls are united in one great divine soul.

The spirit is defined as the expression of the living God: it

*is the principle and essence of everything, including the soul.
The soul represents the possibilities of the spirit. The spirit is
one, but spirits are many: unity and plurality are both
attributes of God. Spirits are as breaths coming from the one
breath. Both spirit and soul need to be expressed in physical
life through the mind, the heart and the will. Spirit and soul
represent the divine which strives to manifest through the
human form as Love, Wisdom and Truth – Life, Light and
Freedom. Mind and heart cannot fully grasp and define the
sublime and majestic nature of the human soul and spirit, but
can be opened to provide for their immediate expression.*

> *Sustain the freedom of your soul,*
> *The strength of your spirit,*
> *The light of your mind,*
> *And the kindness of your heart.*

> *My heart is warm, my soul is fresh,*
> *My mind is light, my spirit is strong,*
> *Because I live in the infinite changeless love of God.*

• • •

CONSCIOUSNESS, SPIRIT AND SOUL

Human beings have been created in the image and likeness
of God. But when people violate the rights of others, they
deviate from the true image and begin to live according to
their own plans and conceptions. Human being deviated
from that image long ago. They have stained that
image – the reason why they recognize neither themselves
nor their neighbours nor God. People today come to earth
with a definite task – that of cleansing the image and
standing pure before their Creator. (27)

God created human beings of two substances: matter, that
is, flesh, and spirit. The flesh, or earth, will always remain
earth. It cannot inherit the Kingdom of God. The divine in
human beings aspires to the great and sublime in life.
When it is said that the spirit never weakens, we mean the
divine and spiritual principle within. The divine never
fails. All impulses and aspirations are due to the divine
within. (3)

No matter how opposed they may be to each other, the life of the spirit and the life of the flesh are necessary for human development. There can be no development or progress without the life of the flesh. Do not be disturbed by the flesh, but try to make it the servant of the spirit. (3)

Seen in themselves, human beings are light. All advanced people who have lived on the earth and who are living now have a special sixth sense which enables them to see others on the inner planes. They see them as candles giving out soft and pleasant light. Goodness is perceived as being radiant, whereas those who have lost the meaning of life are dark. They give out a small, flickering light. (102X)

We can distinguish five categories of people. The world unfolds and follows its path thanks to these different categories of people. The fact of coming to earth means that everyone passes through four of the categories. They begin from the category of ordinary people and gradually go forward.

While people are at the ordinary stage, they buy and sell their food. When they become producers, they pass into the category of talented people. When they become masters of air and water – then they have already become geniuses. And finally, when they become masters of light and darkness, then they will begin to shine and give out light to the whole of humanity. When people have passed through all the categories and become masters of their thoughts – then they begin to see the inner significance of life and pass into the category of Masters. Development within each category is subject to its own facts, laws and theories. (27)

From an astrological point of view, people are divided into different types according to the elements which prevail within them: an earthy type, a Jupiter type, a Mercury type, a Saturn type, a Venus type, etc. Every type represents certain energies within the person. The simpler the person, the fewer the planets that influence them. Great people and geniuses are usually mixed types under the influence of many planets. (27)

Every person represents a special organ in the common organism of nature and has to perform his function. The person who finds his place in nature and realizes his predestined path will be capable of fulfilling his task as an organ of the great divine organism. (25)

You should truly understand what human beings represent: the nature of their aspirations, their thoughts, their feelings and actions, their duties – first of all towards Him who has given them life and the impulse to work in life. Every person who comprehends his position in this fashion and who has a clear image of himself will think correctly, feel correctly and act correctly. (39)

People's stations are determined by their spirits, their souls, their minds and their hearts. They determine their own jobs and life-plans in the world. (32)

What is the task of contemporary people? To help themselves to rise and in this way help the whole of humanity. When a person rises, he is helping his neighbours as well. (26)

The aim of life is this: to realize something immortal on earth, something that will remain in eternity. In this sense every person and every nation can live out something immortal. (56)

Under the present conditions of the entire universe, the boundless universe, this world is one of the best in the sense that there exist all the necessary possibilities and conditions under which we can unfold properly. (64X)

Physical life gives the form of things, spiritual life the content, and the divine their essential meaning. This is the reason why people cannot develop harmoniously without the physical, spiritual or divine life. (14)

The spiritual world is manifested through the spirit, the soul and the body. The physical world, on the other hand, is manifested through the mind, the heart and the will. People are gradually beginning to consider the soul and the spirit as real, and the body as the fruit of their activity. The mind corresponds to the spirit, the heart to the soul, while the will corresponds to the body. (46)

Consciousness

Seeing and creating are two processes of the human spirit.
Every work begins with this. By the word consciousness I
understand the internal regularity which gives life a
coherent meaning. (97X–178)

Consciousness represents the internal organism of human
beings. The soul keeps in touch with the divine world
through it. It is the internal covering of the soul. (56–48)

People find themselves at a higher or lower stage of
development according to the degree of their
consciousness. (56–43)

People are divided into four categories: the first category
contains those who live in their sub-consciousness; the
second category those who live in their consciousness; the
third category those who live in their self-consciousness,
and the fourth category those who live in their
super-consciousness. (97X–205)

The sub-consciousness is a group process which is
concerned with the problems encountered by all spirits.
The consciousness is a group process which deals with the
problems of our friends and neighbours, as well as the
problems of the human race. The self-consciousness is an
individual process which observes the thoughts of every
human being. The super-consciousness is also an individual
process which deals with the thoughts of God. (48–283)

The sub-consciousness is the soul.
The consciousness is the heart.
The self-consciousness is the mind.
The super-consciousness is the human spirit. (86X–291)

The sub-consciousness and the super-consciousness are
two divine poles: one of the poles signifies the human soul
and the other the human spirit. The consciousness and
self-consciousness represent two other poles. One of them
signifies the human heart and the other the human mind.
(97X–203)

The human spirit and the human soul need to be united in
order to find the real path of their development. (86X–291)

The sub-consciousness contains the life of the past. Human experiences are stored there. (84X–158)

The divine law operates in your sub-consciousness. The experiences of past centuries are stored in the sub-consciousness. All the divine laws are gathered there. It is a store of that potential energy. (74X–10)

It is only human beings who store their achievements in their sub-consciousness. (46–30)

You can send an idea to your sub-consciousness and leave it there to grow and unfold. (76X–18)

The internal consciousness of a person, that is, the sub-consciousness, solves the most difficult problems. There is a noetic element in human beings, that is, the divine principle within them. The person who listens to the voice of that principle is always successful. (97X–32)

An idea will be realized if it passes through the sub-consciousness or the super-consciousness. The idea ripens there and then it comes to the world, ready to be realized. (84X–158)

Until the consciousness awakens, people are like unhatched eggs. They are confined in limited conditions, deprived of the light and space of life. (84X–208)

We call 'an awakening of consciousness' the liberation of a person from the limiting conditions of life. (71X–58)

Before the awakening of consciousness, people do not find any meaning in life. (32–370)

People should have an awakened consciousness, differentiating between things so as to discern the beautiful aspects in every shape. (71X–58)

Where is the divine spring? It lies in human consciousness. (46–19)

If you want to keep your consciousness in an awakened state, never allow yourself to entertain bad thoughts about God and the divine world. (23–9)

If a person keeps his consciousness awake to the presence of his spirit, he will be able to cope with the greatest hardships and suffering. (76X)

The more awakened a person's consciousness, the better he is able to resist alien influence. (84X–186)

As soon as consciousness is awakened, you will become aware of your own faults. When you become a conscious person, you will see many things and you will say: 'I should not do this, or that . . .' (86X–264)

When a person decides to correct his faults and wishes well to his neighbour as well as himself, then he has acquired the divine life. That means an awakening of consciousness. (71X–60)

How can people free themselves from murky states of consciousness? They should direct their thoughts to the divine consciousness which permeates the entire cosmos and link themselves with it without any trace of criticism, hesitation or doubt. If people know how to do this, their mood will be pleasant, which will in turn lead to a pleasant feeling; the feelings will become radiant, sublime thoughts. (28–143)

To love God means to give your consciousness the possibility to expand. (71X–89)

In order to expand consciousness, people should regard every event as a part of the whole life, knowing that there is a close and inseparable link between all events. (7–5)

Christ led people out of self-consciousness and directed them towards the divine consciousness, the source of true joy. (58X–276)

Once the divine element is awakened – cosmic consciousness – people begin to lead a sublime and conscious life. (76X–173)

Then that person becomes a spring, and all living beings can avail themselves of their blessing. (76X–214)

When a person's cosmic consciousness is awakened, they

feel an unusual joy, of which nobody can deprive them. (56-73)

When the higher consciousness is awakened within us, we will understand that we have to work for the common good of the whole of humanity, of all living beings - visible and invisible. (42-89)

Humanity is passing into communal consciousness, that is, people begin to realize that they need one another. (65X-26)

Every person living in cosmic consciousness can understand what it means to be in touch with God. (14-29)

May you each witness the moment of being in touch with God. That will give you a stimulus towards attaining the new life, the life of divine cosmic consciousness. (14-29)

The intuition, the divine sense within us, helps us find our orientation in life. (46-143)

Every one of you should try to unfold the divine consciousness, the intuition, so that you may see the divine manifestation of the living Lord of Love in every form. (65X-165)

The disciple has to be awake and correct in his actions. He should never miss the least opportunity for doing something good. This represents a display of the divine consciousness in human beings. (28-49)

Work on yourselves conscientiously and with love, so that you may unfold not only physical but also spiritual power. (71X-229)

No matter how insignificant the person, he contains divine energy within himself. That energy makes him powerful and great. Thanks to this energy he is able to alter his consciousness. (27-64)

If you acquire a new consciousness you have to know how to arrange your life on earth; you will know how to dress, how to eat, what kind of house to build, how to raise your children, and you will know about the methods of educating the whole of society. (39–88)

A day will come when both the flesh and the spirit will live together in the divine. Then all the people will have a new consciousness. They will have a new light, different from what they have now, and will be similar to angels. (39–86)

The more a person grows and develops, the more consciousness grows for the higher worlds: the spiritual and divine. This shows that human consciousness awakens for all the worlds in which life is manifest, although in different forms. (71X–231)

When a person enters the new life, he has to keep his consciousness awake even when he dies; there should be no disconnection of his consciousness. No matter what changes occur, he has to be alert and make use of the changes; he should not lose heart. (27–25)

The conscious work of people in their present lives determines their future. (76X–30)

The present world will pass through great changes that will cause concussions in human consciousness so that people will finally wake up to the fact that they have to be noetic and do the will of God, not their own will. (27–128)

The new consciousness and the new understanding will bring about a radical reform of our entire way of life. (62X–75)

Spirit

The spirit is the beginning of everything. (101X)

That which is born of the flesh is flesh and will die; that which is born of the spirit is spirit and will live throughout eternity. (6)

When the spirit overcomes the flesh, then real life begins. (48)

To be born of the spirit is to be born of the supreme noetic principle of life. To be born of the spirit implies becoming a member of the brotherhood. The brotherhood is a condition of the coming of love among people. (3)

Human beings are living souls, and immortal spirits live within them. We are sent to the world in order to work through those spirits. (48)

Human life springs from the divine spirit. Knowing this, rely on the divine spirit which creates and brings about everything. Follow that spirit which works within you. (26–7)

The soul suffers, the mind becomes confused, the heart may stray from the path of its life, the will may be paralysed; but the spirit never fails. It is the only principle that remains active and strong and repairs the damage that comes about. (55–229)

Which human being knows his spirit and his soul, the spirit that holds the rudder of life? Such a person is master of his thoughts and feelings – he governs himself. He is able to use and apply the knowledge he has received. (32–357)

The power of the human spirit lies in the light and knowledge received. (32–357)

In order to be able to express the energies of your body, you have to sink deeply into substance. So the true human spiritual life will be manifested only after people have been buried in matter and then rise up. (64X–175)

There is a link and relationship between the material and spiritual affairs of human beings. Spiritual affairs reflect the material, and material affairs the spiritual. People's spiritual experience helps them in their spiritual life. (39–76)

The physical body is necessary as a scaffolding on the outside; if it does not rise, neither can the spiritual. (31–130)

The mind and the heart are conditions by means of which the divine spirit is manifested and performs miracles. (3)

The work and efforts of a person's spirit are judged by the degree of development attained by the mind and heart. (56-146)

Therefore the manifestation of our minds, our hearts and our souls at a given moment will show the extent to which we have manifest our spirit. (65X-210)

The human spirit cannot unfold and develop without difficulties. (31-138)

The first requirement for a person to be able to endure suffering, hardships and trials in life is that he should have trained his body. That means that the spirit is present within it. (84X-189)

The divine spirit works from within outwards. It is important for the spirit to begin its work. As soon as the spirit begins to operate from within, it makes outer conditions harmonize with inner ones. The spirit is master of the inner and outer conditions of life. (56-220)

Unless the spirit of God is born within a person, he can neither rise nor follow the proper path of life. He will otherwise have only outer sufferings without any inner ones. (89X-211)

What is the essential thing in life? The freedom of the human spirit. In order to obtain that freedom, a person has to study the laws of life. This is the only way to put aside the limitations which impede the spirit. Only in this way can he restore his inner harmony. (69X-48)

The world in which we live is a great school for training the human spirit. (64X-48)

Do not injure the spirit that leads you in the divine path. You have to learn to reason profoundly in order not to injure the spirit. Do not see things only from one side. Only when you know the profound meaning of things should you express your opinion. Do not ask why God has allowed this or that to happen. (32-76)

What should a person do in order not to fall ill? He has to

feed himself on the fruits of the spirit. If he does not eat these fruits, he will encounter the negative energies of nature and will entertain doubts, suspicion and hatred. (32–149)

Thoughts and feelings which are understood represent fruits in the divine world, and the human spirit feeds on them. (32–43)

If a person wants to be good-looking, to have a pleasant face and bright eyes, he has to know what food to give the spirit. If he feeds it with the appropriate food, he will acquire a physical and spiritual beauty. (32–43)

Growth is a process necessary for the construction of our spiritual body. By the word 'growth' I mean the growing of our spiritual body which represents a unit of the divine harmony. (31–131)

The spirit is the noetic, the powerful principle which leads people to the Kingdom of God. The spirit gives us the greatest gift. The fruit of the spirit is love. If a person has not made contact with the spirit, if he does not eat its fruit, love, he cannot attain the secrets of the divine kingdom. (32–270)

The manifested love of the spirit, the manifested wisdom of the spirit and the manifested truth of the spirit bring the complete life of God, the One, the Eternal God of life. (85X–58)

When the spirit of truth comes, He will instruct you in all things. (3)

The spirit of the Lord and the thought of God must come upon you. This time has come. How can we know it? Only when human beings go to the divine spring with their own vessels to draw of this pure crystal water. (6)

Soul

The spiritual world is linked with the physical: a person exists spiritually and physically at the same time. A link between the two beings joins and governs them. That link is the soul which is semi-spiritual and semi-material. (31X)

The soul is the sub-conscious life. (86X)

The task of a person is to unfold and expand the soul because the experience of the past is stored in it and now the experience of the present is also being stored away. The more the consciousness expands, the richer the soul's experience. (39X)

When we try to uproot evil, we lose all the conditions in which our soul is able to grow, but when we accept things as they are, we grow properly. (40X)

When you find yourselves in difficult situations, talk to your souls – they will help you. (56X)

In the process of learning the value of things, the elements which contribute something to your life or the benefit of your soul at a given moment are the important ones. The good of the human soul is determined by its inner life. The inner life, for its part, is characterized by an inner oneness or inner unity. The unity of things only exists where the will of God is performed. (3)

In order for plants to breathe, they need to be washed. The human soul also needs to be washed if it is to understand the divine. Then life will come. (42)

The human soul must be subjected to the high temperature of the fire of love and to the great pressure of wisdom in order to become divine. (3)

When the soul becomes divine it becomes a diamond reflecting the divine light and forming an aura of delicate tints around itself. Such is the perfect human soul; the human soul aspires towards perfection. (3)

Observe the wise order of the divine soul, in which power precedes freedom, and freedom precedes the radiant thought. Radiant thoughts precede good feelings and good feelings precede good actions. In this way you obtain the happiness you seek. (3)

The soul is the gem within. In it are contained the conditions of human development. Through the soul we come into contact with divine consciousness and begin to work consciously for God. This does not mean giving up one's work. To serve the divine means to know that every action belongs to God and that the eye of God is everywhere and sees everything. When a divine thought occurs to you, accept it and make way for the divine within. (26)

To live for God is to experience one of the most beautiful states of soul. (6)

The soul is the medium in which the spiritual (the real) world is manifest. (46)

Love as a great principle has to penetrate the human soul. (8)

The strength of the human soul lies in the acceptance of love. Such proper acceptance means that peace, joy and gaiety enter the soul and all contradictions disappear. (47)

Every soul which carries within itself the words 'virtue, justice, love, wisdom and truth' is a great and beautiful soul whom everyone is able to love. (38)

There is something in the world which is absolutely free and independent: the first rays of love which illuminate the human soul. (4)

A person's wealth lies in the experience of the soul. (37)

You have to aspire to find your soul. When you find your soul you can see the soul of your neighbour. (7)

Life is meaningful when souls communicate; this shows that human beings represent a common organism. (32)

The spirit is the divine seed within us. The soul is the angelic world within us, like blossom on a tree or plant. The fruit is the human which is revealed through the mind and heart. You cannot speak about the human spirit without understanding the divine. You cannot speak about the soul without understanding the angelic world. You cannot speak about a human being without understanding the mind. The divine, angelic and human life are interrelated in the same way as spirit, soul and mind. (4)

Remember that the royal path of the soul is the good thought of the spirit. (3)

Maintain the freedom of your soul,
The power of your spirit,
The light of your mind,
And the warmth of your hearth. (3)

MIND AND THOUGHT

Few of us are aware of the creative power of the mind to shape our circumstances as well as our inner life. The cultivation of purity, light and love enable it to function effectively and for the good; this also builds a sound mental body and contributes to our physical well-being. The cultivation of these qualities is an essential aspect of our mental life, so much so that meditation on light and harmony is sufficient to bring order and peace into the mind. It is a matter of tuning our instrument to the highest frequency, God, whose resonance naturally aligns and harmonizes us.

• • •

It is the mind that is the creative element in the world; it fashions things and creates beauty. (22X)

The mind is clothed with a specific body – the mental body. It has its own specific organs. People can solve problems of the mind when they develop its organs. (84X)

People study with the mind, acquiring light and knowledge. (19X)

Thought brings light. To be brilliant means to have more light. (25)

The mind should look through the eyes of love. (56X)

Your mind should be always pure and radiant. (6)

If you apply love, the doors of your mind will open and the knowledge of past, present and future will begin to enter in a natural way. You will then become acquainted with the challenges of the new life. (6)

It is sufficient for you to direct your minds and hearts towards new and luminous ideas for them to begin to work within your minds and hearts. Luminous ideas will awaken your higher mental centres. (7X)

The human mind is capable of rarefying or condensing matter and can bring about favourable or unfavourable life circumstances. (7X)

The subjective inner mind is nothing other than a divine principle within human beings. (56X)

The good life begins when the only candles we use are those of our minds. When that candle is burning, we are secure. (13X)

If the mind is sound, so is the health. There are no interruptions in the thought-life of the sound mind. It is not disturbed by anything that happens, because it knows that God is at work everywhere in the world. (6)

When two opposite ideas or principles co-exist in your mind, they split consciousness and you lose your freedom. Never allow your mind to be divided. (17)

When negative thoughts or states arise in you, do not keep them long because they will poison your blood. (13)

The wise person is one who knows God and through whom God manifests. (28)

Wise people have strong powers of thought. (27X)

When feelings are more powerful than thoughts, people become absent-minded and lose their memory. The disciple who wants to strengthen the memory should harmonize his feelings. (76X)

If a person begins to think how much he has grown mentally, he will certainly stumble. (84X)

People feed on light when they accept luminous and radiant thoughts for their minds. The person who properly absorbs light as food has a luminous mind. (32)

My wish is that the minds of all people should be gardens full of sweet and delicious fruit. (32)

Thoughts are constructed by images created by the causal body. (29X)

Thoughts await their moment of manifestation. When will that moment come? When the mind stands in front of the thoughts as their conductor. (46X)

Thoughts and feelings look for conditions in which to manifest, stopping where they find favourable conditions. (6)

Every thought should be poetic and musical. When love, wisdom and truth do not dwell within us, our thoughts do not move smoothly. When a person's thought does not move smoothly, life does not go well. (3)

Every thought should be definite if you want it to be realized. (13)

Thoughts are nourishment. If you do not think, your soul will die of hunger. (4)

Every thought received in the mind must be well chewed, that is, understood and applied. Application is a process of digestion. In digestion, every particle of food is directed to its assigned place. (3)

In order to think straight, we must have light. When the sun rises, the landscape becomes clearly visible; it can be spoken about as well as drawn. Even if you are learned, you can see nothing until the sun has risen, nor can you speak about anything. What the sun represents in the physical world, so does the divine light for human consciousness. As soon as this light penetrates human consciousness, everything becomes clear and visible. A person without this light in consciousness is in total darkness. The person with divine light in consciousness is self-luminous; without this light, one is carrying only a small candle. (3)

The penetration of the smallest divine thought into our lives makes us inwardly independent and develops

within us an inner self-assurance which brings a
little light, a little peace and a little joy. The growth
of this divine thought gradually increases our love,
light, peace and joy. In this moment the whole person
grows. (6)

People should know that they are linked with millions of
other minds on earth and with others not on the earth.
If that link is harmonious the results of their lives will be
good. (56X)

The person should first feel things and then proceed to the
thought. Sublime feelings are a preparation for beautiful
and luminous thoughts. (57–38)

Every thought and every desire that is in harmony with
nature is always accompanied by an expansion and inner
lightness. When people are not in harmony with nature,
they feel an inner constraint, an inner limitation. (18X)

Sound thoughts are those that bring peace to the soul and
light to the spirit. They should provoke the kind of
reaction in people which brings about an expansion of
consciousness. (34X)

Thoughts are powers that move everything. If a person
spends a long time thinking about something, he will
achieve wonders in that direction. If he concentrates for a
long time on getting an object to move, he will be able to
achieve that feat as well. If the thoughts of a person are
continuous, they are able to change the environment.
Thoughts can change the surroundings. There should be a
common link, a continuity, in the thoughts of a person
about a particular problem. (95X–199)

The more intensive the thoughts and feelings of people, the
stronger the light and warmth they radiate. (76X–107)

True and positive thoughts are only such as are beneficial
to people and those around them. (28–47)

Good thoughts and feelings promote long life. (38–37)

No matter what may come your way, keep positive
thoughts in your heads. (38–97)

You should create new thoughts. It is not enough to repeat
established ones. Repeating things does not lead to
knowledge. (28–275)

If you do not fling old ideas out of your mind, you cannot
give birth to new ones. (31–84)

Every thought is strong until you put it into words.
(77X–20)

Keep only pure and radiant thoughts in your mind.
Stay away from evil thoughts and desires. They not only
leave a stain on people's faces, but they attract bad things
to themselves. (58–150)

Thoughts – both good and bad – circulate around the
person who has created them. People sometimes wonder
how certain thoughts have entered their mind. They have
no inkling that these thoughts are the very ones that they
have projected into space. (95X–207)

Every person who thinks – who deals in serious
thoughts – has more light in their head than the person
who does not think. Light is linked with truth, while truth
is the stimulus of wisdom. We seek truth by means of
wisdom. So light is the result of motions taking place
within the human brain. Seekers of truth have more light
within them. (69X–30)

If you wish to arrive at the correct solution of a problem,
stop dwelling on it. Be passive with respect to your worries
and troubles, so as to be able to accept a positive thought
from the higher world. Such a thought will help you solve
your problem correctly. This is the natural way to solve
problems. (28–79)

When you learn the art of correct thinking, you will
liberate yourselves from your present state; everything
around you will change and you will see the world in a
new light. (24)

The power of a divine thought lies in its application.
The applying of one thought in your life means that you
have realized that it is true. (6–35)

No thoughts can be realized without the participation of the feelings. Thoughts provide the shape, while feelings give the impetus. (92X)

Feelings represent the roots of the tree and thoughts the branches. (58X–266)

Your thoughts will be able to operate like a dynamic energy if you link yourselves with the spiritual world. (31–174)

Each thought has to be planted so that it may grow and bear fruit. (64X–173)

A definite gestation period is required for the realization of human thoughts and desires. If that period is either prolonged or shortened, the possibilities of realization are lost. (18–80)

How can a person help himself in his life? By means of thought. When he thinks, he will free himself from his prevailing bad conditions. (58X–243)

People can make use of suggestion to enhance health, develop capacities, increase their powers of memory, etc. No matter what your circumstances, bear in mind the positive thought that you will be able to find a favourable soil for continuing your work. (76X–88)

Good thoughts maintain the brain in a sound state. (32–127)

Think intensively, but do not worry. (83X–122)

Spend five minutes every day thinking about eternal life, God, good people, good mothers and fathers, good friends. Thinking about noble things will elevate your mind. (31–79)

People should keep their thoughts and desires sacred because such are the paths which link them to the divine world. (6–35)

Human thoughts have great power. They penetrate everywhere and change things imperceptibly. (84X)

HEART, FEELINGS AND DESIRES

If the highest expression of the mind is light and wisdom, that of the pure heart is love. Since love is itself the heart of Beinsa Douno's message, the cultivation of the feelings and desires of the heart is essential spiritual work, all the more so since his vision of the new culture is a culture of love, of the heart. Just as thoughts need to be directed and organized, so do feelings and desires through the nurturing of nobility and purity.

> God created the earth for us to be good,
> Water for us to be pure,
> Air for us to think correctly,
> And light for us to walk on the right path.

● ● ●

Heart

In the scripture it is written: My son, give me your heart. God does not want your mind, but your heart. When you give God your heart, you will have life abundant. (42)

Direct all your energies and efforts towards the ennoblement of your heart. The new culture will be a culture of the heart. Then people will feel like brothers and sisters. They will live a life of brotherhood; love will be revealed to the heart. (25)

It is said of the human body that it is the temple of God. The hearth of that temple is the heart, where the fire is constantly burning. (81X–80)

The heart is the place where the springs of life are constantly flowing in and out. (76X–115)

The heart is linked to the cosmos and draws vital energies from it. (27–270)

The more generously a person opens his heart to small, weak and feeble creatures, the more he is given. (71X–17)

It is said: 'Blessed are the pure in heart, for they shall see God.' (146X)

People should have pure hearts. The pure heart is a spring: the more it gives, the more flows out of it. (71X–177)

To be a good person means having a well-organized heart. (76X–77)

A good and harmonious heart sympathizes with every suffering person. (79X)

When God influences my heart, it is gentle. I say, 'Come, my friend, I am ready to share my bread with you.' (83X–22)

A heart in which the secret fire is burning represents a spring of noble and sublime feelings and thoughts. (56–183)

Human talents and abilities develop properly under the influence of that fire. (27–117)

The vitality which radiates from a person is due to his noble heart. Such a person cannot help being loved. The face of such a person shines. (76X–75)

A heart-centred person is one in whose soul there reigns an eternal spring. (91X–11)

When the heart feels properly, the soul is sound. It is the heart that prepares food for the soul. (84X–8)

Sublime beings bring sublime impulses, noble feelings and desires into our hearts. (46–202)

Life is meaningful when a person's heart is full of love. (27–82)

If a person does not make room for God in his heart, he blocks his own path in life. (27–76)

Always listen to the voice of your heart and walk along its paths. The divine laws are written in the heart. (27–336)

May every heart be a pure spring which flows ceaselessly. (32–375)

Feelings

As the stomach needs food, so the heart needs feelings. (46–228)

Feelings are an expression and conductor of noetic energy projected in nature. (97X–626)

Feelings collect the energy which the mind uses. (43–111)

When a person feels something, his feelings are simultaneously making the blood circulate. When the feelings are positive they make arterial blood circulate and give rise to positive thoughts. (2–25)

Divine feelings whisper to people what is right and what is not. They provide an orientation in the field of high morals which enables them to be sound, powerful and stable in resisting all storms and trials. (27–268)

If a person's feelings are not correctly shaped, his mental conclusions and deductions will be incorrect. (39–63)

One of the basic feelings of a disciple is sympathy with all living beings and the knowledge that they also suffer at least as much as he does. (43–300)

Feelings without love serve no purpose. (91X–57)

Moral and social feelings develop suppleness. (18–176)

People cannot reach profundity of feelings without any suffering; and without joy, feelings cannot expand. The greater the depth and width of people's feelings, the more extensive the possibilities which open up in their mental lives. (76X–120)

People should keep their consciousness aware and link themselves with the sublime and noetic beings in order to protect themselves from negative feelings. (84X–34)

People will be invincible from outer conditions when they unfold their inner feelings and capacities. They will then be able to foretell events. (27–161)

As disciples you have to work upon yourselves to unfold divine feelings. (21–312)

Whatever you are doing, whatever your work – make use of it to develop tender and noble feelings within your hearts. (43–315)

Desires

What is a desire? An energy collected within a person which wishes to manifest itself. (16–78)

Desires are food for the heart. (27–185)

To kill desires means to annihilate your hearts. (27–185)

Strong desires stimulate people's cells and organs, directing them to a certain activity. (84X–52)

Strong desires determine the future of humanity. (76X–196)

People's desire to grow and rise is not a temporary one; it is a desire that has existed from time immemorial. (76X–214)

Every natural desire has to be fulfilled. They stimulate people. Natural desires are noetic. (84X–47)

If a person desires something useless for himself, he has already introduced some poison into his system, a poison which will demolish him. (71X–214)

People are always susceptible to alien desires left over from past ages. (84X–182)

Every insatiable desire for glory, wealth and knowledge is nothing other than a remnant of the desires of antediluvian animals. In order to cope with such a desire, people should find another desire which corresponds to the first and pour the energy of the antediluvian desire into the new desire. (84X–193)

Go to the divine spring and receive directly that desire which is intrinsically related to your soul. Where is the divine spring? It is within one's consciousness. Rise to acquire new and sublime desires in your consciousness. (46–17)

People must have strong desires, but not many of them. (84X–52)

When it is said that people should not have many desires, this means that they must free themselves from the burdens of life. The law is not to desire what may crush you. (71X–167)

You bring misfortunes on yourselves through your inordinate desires. That is why you must learn how to withhold these desires. If you want to realize a great many of your desires you thus enslave yourselves. (85X–8)

In order for a person not to damage his talents, he has to give up unnecessary and fruitless desires – that is why discrimination is required – people should know which desires have to be retained and which set aside. The latter are manure for their lives. (76X–110)

If an unnatural desire enters your heart, do not struggle with it – but look for a way of getting rid of it. (46–20)

We must make all our feelings and desires pass through our minds – through the prism of our minds. (50–4)

People who live in accordance with the laws of nature realize their desires. (27–42)

In order to realize any of your desires, you need to be linked with God. (97X)

People can achieve all that they desire; but they need an alert consciousness and have to work conscientiously on themselves. (56–122)

We can achieve everything in life – but at the appointed time. There is a right moment for everything – but we must be alert and on the look-out for the appointed moment. (38–48)

It is sufficient for people to open their hearts to divine feelings and their minds to divine thoughts in order to be able to achieve their desires. (27–187)

A sublime desire acts as a link with the consciousness of higher beings who help in the realization of that desire.

The person then lives in the consciousness of the light of those beings. (76X–51)

As disciples you must have patience and resilience so as to achieve the desires of your souls. (76X–98)

The realization of one's desires requires faith. (98X–17)

When a strong noetic desire speaks within you, do not block it. Give it a chance to manifest itself. The results of the realization of good desires are always good, but they need to be enacted at the right time and according to a well thought-out plan. (46–78)

If a person wants to achieve something, he has to direct the desire to his mind in the form of a thought; then he should begin to realize it in the physical world. (76X–53)

In the realization of desires the law says that you must put it into your sub-conscious mind and not give it any more thought. Then work in that direction without thinking about when the desire will be realized and what the results will be. (84X–53)

Put a seed in the soil and it will show you how to achieve your desires. (27–112)

It is not sufficient for a person to have desires; they should be organized, that is, they should know why they desire this or that, how it can be realized and what the result of a given desire is going to be. (46–23)

Your great desire should be for a luminous mind that carries light, a heart full of warmth that will help things to grow. You should ask for the kind of heart that will help the growth of all divine ideas. You should ask for a will-power that will overcome all hardships. You have to live in a world reigned over by light and warmth – then you will achieve everything you desire. (38–76)

If your desire is divine, carry it out without thinking about other people's opinions. Do not think that your human desires are divine because you will then bring misfortune upon yourselves. (39–83)

The situation of a person in the grave is difficult if they have not put most of their desires aside, that is, if they have not severed their links with the earth. People who have worked consciously and have done away with their earthly desires will easily liberate themselves from their bodies. (27–391)

WILL

The will is the third part of the triangle of mind and heart. The ideal of the disciple is a balanced development of all three faculties, represented by the equilateral triangle. Much of the impulse of the New Age has been from the heart, often at the expense of mind and will. Without the will, we lack the strength, courage and perseverance to carry our projects through to fruition. In recommending methods of reinforcing the will, Beinsa Douno often integrated spiritual and physical exercises, as in the climbing of peaks in the Rila mountains or in combining physical gestures with spiritual formulas. It will be seen below that there are different levels of will – mental, emotional and physical – each of which needs to be exercised and have a reciprocal influence on the other.

•   •   •

The will gives stability, courage and effectiveness. (22)

When you develop your will, you will realize all your desires. In order to do this, begin with small things, small ideas. (48)

To strengthen your will you have first to develop good habits. (28)

To do good requires will. In order to progress in life you must have a will. You can rise only in and through the good. Will is not necessary in doing evil: you simply step into its stream and it pulls you downward. Will is necessary for the doing of good. (20)

The strength of a person is determined by the quality of will-power. (9–49)

The will-power is a force, an energy that does everything. It is the result of thoughts and desires. (10–78)

The mind is a person's positive energy, while the heart is negative energy. The will-power, however, is neutral. If your will-power is not strong you cannot regulate the energies of mind and heart. (58X–226)

Will-power is the result of the productive work of mind and heart that have walked along a new path and worked in accordance with the divine law. (95X–47)

The will manifests in the three worlds: in the mental, in the emotional – the world of feelings and desires or so-called astral world – and in the physical world. (25–33)

The person who persists even if he has received ninety-nine refusals is one with will-power. His will-power will prevail at the hundredth effort. (25–70)

Will-power is expressed in people's hands, feet, tongue and eyes. The senses are repositories of will-power. It manifests and operates through the senses. (25–36)

Every person has some work to do. He has to deal with the matter of his own body. People have billions of cells in their bodies; they should govern them noetically and consciously. Every cell has its own comprehension and people have to coordinate the lives of all cells, to organize them and subject them to one common great and noetic will. (27–248)

For the conscious person hardships are conditions for unfolding the will-power. (76X–161)

People begin to develop only when they meet impediments to their will. (4–34)

You will be given some impossible things to do – if you overcome them this shows that you have will-power and are capable of awakening those hidden occult energies within yourselves and make them work. (94X–9)

Somebody offends you. If you are able to overcome the offence you have will-power. (77X–7)

People are only now beginning to work with their noetic will-power. For a person to display noetic will they have to organize their thoughts, feelings and actions. (46–23)

People can practise strengthening their will in small things. (25–38)

Some beings do the will of God, other beings do their own will. (32–69)

One of the tasks of disciples is to govern their minds and hearts, that is, their own thoughts and feelings, their energies and capacities. They have to be under the control of the noetic will-power. (95X–113)

When a person makes up his mind to do something, he should immediately go about realizing it. Do not put anything off. When your desires are good, start realizing them straight away. (18)

A person's development of good habits is the first condition for strengthening the will-power. (58X–8)

If you can fall asleep at a definite time, your will-power is strong. The will-power is tested only in exercises. To strengthen your will-power when you go to bed at night, say to yourself that you would like to sleep only on your right side. If you find yourself on your right side in the morning, then your will-power is strong; if you find yourself on your left side, your will-power is weak. But that should not discourage you. Do these exercises until you obtain good results. (25–33)

What kind of will-power do you have to attain? It should not be an iron one, nor a granite one – it should be a diamond will-power. (81X–88)

Few people have placed the noetic will-power as a foundation to their lives, that is, the noetic will-power governed by love. (95X–143)

The strength of a person's will-power depends on the strength of their thoughts and desires. The stronger the images of human thoughts and desires, the more active the will-power. (18–106)

When you work on your will-power, you firstly deal with the physical person – the body, then with your feelings and, thirdly, with your thoughts. This is the only way by which you can reconstruct your bodies and bring into them those elements which will give them more buoyancy and resilience; only thus will you introduce a greater tenacity to the feelings and a greater strength to the thoughts. (25–40)

Summary on Mind, Heart and Will

The human mind creates. The human mind makes contacts. (27)

When the mind is full of doubts, that is not thought. A heart which worries and a mind which doubts do not achieve anything. Place a noble feeling in your heart and a luminous thought in your mind and let them be. (3)

The powerful desires, thoughts and feelings which emerge from the depth of your soul are divine springs. Do not place any obstacles on the path of divine impulses. (42)

Wealth and power are qualities of the human mind and heart. The dynamo which directs the mind and heart and uses their wealth and power is the human will. (6)

The heart cannot solve the problems of life: the mind must be put to work. As soon as the mind starts working, the heart must unite as its partner. (6)

It is inexcusable for a person who has been given a fine mind and heart not to behave properly and appreciate the qualities of his neighbour. This is why every person has to work out the right kind of behaviour for himself and an appreciative feeling for small things. As this feeling is developed, so are one's inner attitudes. The person without the right outer and inner behaviour clashes with the divine will. Every discontent and every indisposition is due to breaking the law of right relation and evaluation of small things. It is not enough to have only a right external relation to things, but the same must be done within, that is, to love all living beings and treat them as one would treat oneself. (3)

Thoughts are the capital of the mind, feelings are the capital of the heart and actions the capital of the will. People are rich but responsible for the use of their wealth. (3)

When a person thinks correctly he is in the divine world; when he feels correctly he is in the spiritual world; when he acts correctly he is in the physical world. If, however, you do not think, feel and act correctly, you are expelled from the corresponding world and forfeit your rights of citizenship. (14)

To accept the divine does not mean to give up life. You have to live in order to apply the divine and do the will of God. In this way we set our minds and hearts to rights; when people do this, the world will be set to rights. (26)

Everyone has to work on his mind, heart and will, whether he is simple or learned, servant or ruler, poor or rich. The goods of life are for all, the rights of one are the rights of all. (18)

Remember to maintain the balance of your mind, heart and will no matter what happens in life. (3)

Every thought, feeling and action in all its manifestations should be absolutely pure. (3)

It is a good thing to be influenced by your feelings, but you must first have a noble heart. Nobility will prevent you from sliding down that slope of purely personal feeling. Human beings should be perfect in feelings, thoughts and actions; they will then be careful with every word they say. (3)

Every thought, every feeling and every action has to pass through the mind, the heart and the will in order to be filtered. Only after this filtering can they be planted in the garden of the soul. (18)

HUMAN CONDUCT

The overall context of human conduct is the whole of creation and in that context we are an integral part of the whole and are therefore in relationship with the lives of all creatures. This is a central moral insight. A morality based on love leads naturally to giving, sacrifice and mutual aid: good actions are the direct expression and outcome of love. Conduct is also the ultimate materialization of qualities of mind, heart and will, the touchstone of inner development.

> You should first of all love the whole;
> By loving the whole you will love the
> parts.
> When you attain cosmic love, you
> love all beings
> Because the unity of life is real to you.

• • •

You cannot be moral if you live only for yourself. You are not even moral if you live for others. Truly moral is that person who lives first for God, for the whole creation. (96X–163)

While a person is living only for himself, he is in limited conditions of activity; when he lives for other people, the conditions become richer; if he arrives at the ideal understanding of life, the fulfilment of divine laws, he enters the fullness of life which comprises everything. (7–5)

Strive towards the supreme morality which considers the interests of the lives of all creatures. (27–296)

No connection can exist between people if they are not permeated by the desire to help one another – in their thoughts, feelings and actions. (34–102)

Before approaching a person, the first thing to do is to find a good characteristic, either in their minds or hearts: an essential motivating thought, a noble feeling or inherent capacity. (60X–25)

There exists a law of nature concerning relationships

between forms, powers and energies. They can be noetic or the reverse, harmonious or disharmonious. When relations are noetic and harmonious, we can see growth everywhere in life. (71X–146)

Link yourselves with the souls with whom you are in harmony. (72X–1)

In order for people to grow and unfold correctly, they should link themselves with at least one advanced soul every day. (72X–15)

Three things are important in people's lives: to serve God, to respect themselves and to love their neighbours. (3–12)

Do not expect people to love you – love them first. (90X–328)

When you meet a person, think well of them. Tell yourself that they have excellent thoughts and the finest feelings within; that they have an excellent soul and an excellent spirit. If you think of people in this way, they will respond in kind. (38–22)

If you are noetic and see to the good of your neighbours as you see to your own good, everyone will love you: your relations, your friends, society and so on. (27–201)

We refer to the law of love as a link between souls. The law of love demands mutual aid between human beings. (72X–17)

When two people love each other, they have to direct their energies to a third centre, common to them both. Otherwise, if they leave their energies simply flowing between them, they will crash, explode and lose themselves in space. (28–268)

When the consciousness of two beings is aware, they sacrifice themselves at the right moment, they serve each other and they do the will of God at the right time. (28–49)

Noetic people try to have a correct attitude to the people around them. They are careful in their thoughts, feelings and actions; they try not to cause any harm to their dear ones or to themselves. (20–23)

Wherever there is harmony and love between souls, there exists companionship and true friendship. (95X–249)

Two people can be friends if they have three common points: in the physical, in the spiritual and in the divine worlds. (87X–224)

When two friends become close, their astral bodies link and the energies begin to flow from one to the other. (17–26)

Friends are only people who are willing to sacrifice themselves for your growth. (25–63)

You will recognize your friends in times of suffering. (86X–51)

If people really respected each other and were prepared to give way, then there would be great harmony in life. (31–118)

Let us be ready to help one another at all difficult moments and whenever there are hard tasks to perform. (82X–221)

Rendering a service is a manifestation of the divine element within us. (103X–63)

Help every person without liberating them from their trials. (85X–84)

When you live you have to think of others and make sacrifices. It is impossible without sacrifices. By the word *sacrifice* we mean a noetic process. Our sacrifice gives us power and resilience. To sacrifice means to do the most noetic thing in one's life. (85X–134)

The person who gives has to be sensitive, responsive – they should understand the needs of others and help them before they request it. (45–221)

Love should partake in giving – to open human hearts; wisdom and truth should also take part – to give scope to the human will, so that people may willingly do the will of God. (27–384)

If you are a spring which is flowing all the time, people will always visit you - you will never be left alone. If you are a spring that gives in a disinterested way, your life will definitely flow along the correct path. (18-33)

The good person is an expression of the noetic will of God. (97X-101)

Good deeds are nothing other than love expressed in the physical world. (34-107)

It is not easy to be good. It is an art to know how and where you should perform a good deed. (95X-294)

It is not sufficient to do a good deed - but it has to be done at the right time and in the right place. (45-216)

When we come to the state of giving we should always feel joy within our heart that we have done the will of God. (95X-50)

A good deed is only what has been done with our own hands. That is why you should learn to work and give something away from the fruits of your own labour. (83X-43)

If you want to do a good deed, do not do it without love. (83X-50)

The good deed is different from the bad one because it always builds and creates, while the evil deed destroys. (83X-63)

Even the smallest good deed you have done is able to bring you more benefit than the greatest knowledge. (85X-160)

People should do a good deed every day - expressed either in a thought, a feeling or an action. Such a good deed can be done to a spring, to a plant, to a fly or to a human being. No matter how small the good deed, it has to be done. (45-177)

To give meaning to giving and taking, people have to be thankful. The energy that flows from the person who gives and the person who takes is a divine energy and an account is being kept of it. It cannot and should not be used in vain. Nature has exact instruments which register the amount of energy and the person for whom it has been spent. (25-114)

Every human thought, every human feeling and every human action has to express gratitude to God, to all those radiant sublime beings that have bestowed the good things. (28-183)

One thing is essential: people should realize that the world created by God is a good one and they should be grateful for everything that has been given to them. (87X-150)

If we are grateful for the small good thing, the greater one will come. If we are not grateful for the small evil, a greater one will come. (87X-310)

Human happiness lies in freedom. Every person who enslaves brings misfortune. Every person who liberates brings happiness. (89X-322)

I have no right to order about or misuse the things belonging to others. I have the right only to be the master of my own thoughts and desires. Only I can order them about. However, I should serve everything else which is outside me. (31-120)

Do not express your opinion about people because you are doing so about the work of God. You do not know what God is going to do with those people. God has not finished his work on them. There is no worse thing than to look for the faults of other people. It is another thing, though, if you are ready to pay for them. (38-47)

Do not criticize one another. Look for each person's good characteristics. (90X-416)

When a person learns from the mistakes of other people without judging them, he retains their love. (32-162)

Every person is an object-lesson. Whether you like him or

not, you should neither judge nor praise him, you have to learn something from him. (90X–116)

It is better for you alone to judge yourself and correct your mistakes than to let others judge you or correct them for you. (28–148)

If you do not forgive a person, you will hold him in your mind together with his sin and that will contaminate you. (89X–21)

The tongue of a person should become so soft that every word which passes through it sounds harmonious to the human ear. (95X–237)

If you say something to a person and you feel joy in your mind, then what you have said is true. (49–14)

When you say something good about a person, you gain, and when you say something bad about them, they gain. Such is the law. (31–95)

People create their future through their mouths. If you speak noetically, you are preparing a bright future for yourselves. (26–40)

All sins and crimes of a person can be forgiven but the lie – never. It is the smallest evil from which all other evils spring. (54–30)

If you promise something, you may meet 100 bears on your path, but you must keep your promise. (28–5)

Don't put things off. Always be aware and make use of favourable circumstances in life; because every thought, every idea and every truth can be given at a definite time. (95X–139)

Punctuality is a harmony, a measure, music in human life. (28–163)

The first condition of a noetic life is punctuality. If you are not punctual, you cannot realize your desires. (46–175)

All people should work conscientiously, willingly and with love – without any forcing. (56–129)

Joy is the first manifestation of love. If you love someone, you feel glad. If they love you, they feel glad. Apart from joy everything is second-hand. (26-209)

Be enthusiastic about what you have: be inspired by your mind that brings light. Rejoice in the warmth of your heart. Rejoice at your soul which has been carrying divine blessings for thousands and millions of years. Rejoice in your spirit that leads you along the path to God. Why should you get discouraged? Rejoice in everything that has been given you and live according to divine law. (32-17)

When people are glad, they sing – although they may not be singers, they sing inwardly. (80X-6)

I should like to have from each of you, first of all, the most tender feeling, the softest glance and the sweetest word. (79X-18)

Be grateful for what has been given you. What greater wealth do you expect than the wealth of your mind and heart? What greater wealth do you expect than the wealth of your soul and your spirit? Such wealth cannot be compared with the wealth of any king on earth. (32-15)

You must become living eyes, living ears and living mouths for the manifestation of divine love, divine wisdom and divine truth. Only thus will life, knowledge and freedom come. (32-113)

Marriage is a law of self-sacrifice so that you may attain purity or pay your karma, as people in India say. (86X-285)

Value your mind, heart and will. Act well towards your neighbour, towards all plants and animals, towards the whole of nature. Value everything that surrounds you. If you do this, you will be a disciple of the new life, a disciple of love. (3)

If you want to harmonize the life of the mind, the heart, the will, the soul and the spirit, make the idea of brotherhood and friendship the basis of your life. (16)

If the human heart is not pure, if the mind is not sacred, if the will is not strong and if the soul is not full of love, the word human has no sense. (3)

It is a mistake to think that ideas are to be applied outside oneself. Whatever one can apply should be applied within – nowhere else. Only what is applied generates light. People's desire to apply their ideas outside themselves will never be an attainable ideal. When the Primary Principle created the world He applied everything within Himself. That is why it is written: 'All things move and have their being in God.' God applies everything within Himself, but we want to bring them out and apply them outside ourselves. What greater contradiction can there be than this? As a result of this contradiction, people collide with the divine order of things. (3)

THE PHYSICAL BODY

If Christianity began with ascetic and other-worldly tenden- cies, these were taken to an extreme by dualist heretics (see Introduction) who considered matter and the body as evil. Such an attitude has encouraged unfortunate excesses such as flagellation and self-mutilation, thus leading to a partial or total misunderstanding of the nature and func- tion of the physical body. Beinsa Douno describes it as an outward representation of the person's character; he lays great emphasis on the need to look after it, as we shall see in his recommendations for life. The body is likened to a temple or dwelling in which we study during our sojourn on earth. This, however, is only one level, since we shall need other bodies and faculties of perception in order to operate in other worlds.

The physical body is the outcome of a person's activity. (9X)

Human culture depends on the organization of their bodies. The body is the result of the human spirit. A day will come when the spirit will create immortal human bodies. (58X)

Our body is the temple of God. (6)

All a person's organs are fashioned in accordance with character and soul. (22)

The human organism is a great country in which the citizens are united in the name of love. This love acts over a period of millions of years to organize all cells into a united whole to do common work. Whoever realizes this and can maintain a great harmony in their organism can enjoy good health and a happy life. (32)

People need to understand the forces operating inside and outside themselves in order to balance these and employ them constructively towards a creative life. (14)

Human beings on earth are given conditions and possibilities to help them in their development.
The human organism is the first condition which is given to us as students. The human body represents the building, school or university in which they are placed to study. (14)

When you study anatomy and physiology you make contact with the physical and spiritual function of the organs. Every organ has both functions – external and internal – that is, material and spiritual. (31)

The physical body possesses not only physical organs which are necessary for the physical world. It also has other organs which are necessary for other worlds.
So while people are working for the development of their physical organs, they are also working towards developing their mental and spiritual organs. They will otherwise only be fit for the physical world. If they go to the spiritual world, they will be in the position of new-born babes who need the help of their relatives. (27)

The human body is a synthesis of all processes in nature. If you know your body, you will also know the invisible world. (50)

The occult disciple should work towards the purification of the body. (6)

Beautiful is that face in which every change of thought, feeling and action can be noticed. In spite of of the continual changes of facial expression, there are traits in such a face which remain the same. Such a face is an expression of a noble and elevated soul. Beautiful is that person whose face you can read. The beautiful face manifests everything that lies hidden in the soul. Beautiful is the face on which God writes, while the human being maintains the purity of what is inscribed. (6)

7

Methods, Rules and Recommendations for Life

The knowledge of a Master embraces both natural and spiritual laws which have been tested through personal insight and experience. The methods and rules given are all means of working on oneself and can only be truly understood through disciplined practice.

When I speak to you, I give certain laws and rules by which you should live. I speak to you about human beings: what human ideals have been like in the past and what people must be like in the future. (6)

I say: These rules which I give you are sacredly to be guarded by each person for himself. Apply them, observe the results and then recommend them to other people. If you recommend them to others before you have tested them yourself, they will lose their effect and power. (6)

You say: How can I work? What methods should we apply in studying? I say: Observe nature and see how she works and learn from her. Use her methods in your own development. (6)

The only methods which cause no ill-effects are those operating through the laws of Love, Wisdom and Truth. They are the only pure methods by means of which we can act. (77X)

When a person has come to earth, they have to seek out not only mountain peaks to climb in the physical world,

but peaks in the spiritual field for spiritual growth.
Hence the need to select appropriate methods for working
on oneself. (7X)

The new is important – the new that you are
understanding at present, the new that you are able to
work out and apply in your present life. (97X)

When you are afraid of doing something – do it, and the
fear will vanish. (106X)

A regulation to use when you are overcome by anger or
irritation – sing C, E, G, C (the higher C) ten times, and
your anger will pass. (25X)

Observe the following rule: if you solve a problem
correctly, a little light begins to shine in your mind,
bringing some joy into you. If there is no light when you
solve the problem, it has not been solved correctly.
This rule can be applied everywhere, in life as in science.
(28)

Bear in mind the idea that the world is good but a change
must take place in human conceptions. When such an
alteration takes place in the mind and conceptions,
the external world will change. Therefore, the
transformation of the world requires some conscious
inner work on the part of all. (51)

DAILY PRACTICE

In Daily Practice, *the reader will find advice specific to a time
of day, but also recommendations which can be carried out
as the occasion arises and constant injunctions to maintain an
inner link with God and the higher world. Every day brings
new opportunities for growth. More specific aspects of daily
activity are covered under separate sections in this chapter.*

In The Circle of Sacred Dance *I have described life in the
Rila camp in more detail; at present, this is the only period of
the year when a regular communal life is possible. The camp
is woken at 5 am by the haunting melody 'Stani' ('Arise'). We
drink a cup of hot water before climbing the mountain to*

witness the sunrise. We meditate in silence and then, as the sun rises, we make a salute with our right hands, before singing some songs and saying a few prayers and formulas. Before breakfast we perform the six and twenty-two gymnastic exercises and dance the paneurhythmy. All meals are eaten communally, and each person takes it in turn to be on duty for a twenty-four hour period. Other jobs may be done together during the day, depending on circumstances. In the evening there is always a camp fire around which the musicians play and we all sing some more of the Master's songs. Finally comes the evening prayer, a precious moment before we retire to our tents.

●　　●　　●

Keep in your mind the positive thought that whatever happens to you during the day is for your good. (3)

What should be your first thought when you get up?
Say: 'Bless my soul, God. I thank Thee that I have risen today to do the work I should do and may I grow as much as I should.' (31X)

When you get up in the morning, say: 'God is Love.' (115X)

Give thanks to God for everything that has been given you. (38X)

When you wake up in the morning and before you wash your face, call the best feeling in your heart and say the first word of love to it. Call the most beautiful thought in your mind and show it the prettiest light! Having done this, pronounce the following sacred formula:
'Merciful, sacred and kind God, show me the light of Thy face so that I may do Thy will.' One of the rules in saying a formula is that you should be very positive and have the spirit of a child when pronouncing it. (122X)

When you get up in the morning, you may say the formula (three times), repeating it at noon and in the evening: 'God has invested everything in my soul. I want to do the will of God, I want to fulfil God's plan. Whatever God has planned for me, may His will be done. I am going to work as God has determined.' (106X)

You should be aware that every person represents a society composed of noetic souls that have something in common with them. Therefore, when you get up in the morning, your first job is to harmonize these noetic little beings. You have to restore the harmony of your whole body. This is achieved by means of prayer, concentration and work. (76X)

In the morning, before you start doing anything, stretch your spine so that the currents of nature may circulate properly. Then send your thoughts to the invisible world, make contact with God and then get up to begin your work. You will not be able to succeed in your work before you have adjusted your nervous system. (114X)

The disciple should never hurry. Dressing and washing can be left till later. Your first task is five or ten minutes in meditation thinking of God and all the advanced beings, calling them to your assistance, saying, 'Lord, I have little knowledge, enlighten my mind to accept and do Thy will. Show me a way in which I may realize Thy wishes as Thou hast determined.' If you say this, you will receive the answer to your prayer a little later. You will feel a peace in your soul, a certain joy, and then you will start your work. If you act in this way, there will be harmony within your soul which will help you in your work. (114X)

Say to yourselves, 'I am contented as I am created at present. There are some capacities that I have to unfold and develop. I will study and work towards acquiring something to add to my present wealth.' (46)

Strive towards the greatest, the most beautiful, the best and the purest. That is the truth which you have to place in your souls, hearts and minds. (13X)

Every day has its own programme. If disciples carry out their daily programme as they should, the programmes of their entire lives would be accomplished properly. (27X)

Every day brings its own blessing. (21X)

There is a definite rhythm for speaking, walking and acting. Human beings should observe these rhythms established by nature herself. (56X)

Reflect that the first day – the day of your spirit – is a day on which light is manifest. Reflect that the second day – the day of your soul – is a day on which love is manifest. Reflect that the third day – the day of your mind – is a day on which knowledge is manifest. Reflect that the fourth day – the day of your heart – is a day on which conscious life is manifest. Reflect that the fifth day – the day of your will-power – is a day of your energies – the energies that have come to help you. Reflect that the sixth day is the day of the eternal word which has illuminated you and made you the master of your fate. The seventh day is a day that belongs to God – the Eternal Principle – a day of learning from nature, a day of rest when you serve all virtues. (38X)

On Sunday you should not weep, wash your clothes or take money from your debtors. On Sunday you should take a sack of flour to a poor widow, cure an ill person, comfort an unhappy person, place a new thought in your mind. You are allowed to light the fire of your heart on Sunday, to light a new fire in your body, a fire that will bring you health and peace. On Sunday you have to be a candle to God. (106X)

People who serve God avail themselves of fresh air, light, food and all other good things in life. There are no bad days for them, there are no bad conditions, there is no bad weather. (21X)

Do not wait for external conditions to improve. Conditions have been good ever since the world began but people have not been prepared to make good use of them. (21X)

Life is eternal growth and development. (97X)

Life is not static but dynamic: yesterday's happiness cannot be today's; and your present happiness cannot warm your heart tomorrow. The present day requires new conditions. Every day and every minute we should apply something new in life. If you do not introduce anything new into your lives, you will lose what you have got. (97X)

Nowadays, people grow old before their time because they hurry everywhere – in their eating, in their movements, in their studying. They want to have a quick success; when they begin something, they want to finish it in haste. (90X)

If a person makes a reasonable use of every day and every hour, he will realize his desires in the course of two years. No hurry is necessary, however. One should be constant and stable in one's work. (34X)

If one wants something great for oneself, one has to pay the respective price for it. Nature does not give anything free of charge. (34X)

Before going to bed at night, spend ten or fifteen minutes reviewing how you have spent the day and see what mistakes you have made. Mentally put your faults right, take a few deep breaths and, when you are calm, go to bed. Your sleep will be good and energizing. (21X)

People should wash their feet every evening in warm water. (21X)

Every evening when you go to bed and every morning when you get up, say, 'Everything is possible.' (13X)

The best time for going to bed is 10 pm, but that cannot be taken as a rule. The earlier you go to bed the better. The people who go to bed early absorb all the prana, that is, all the living energy gathered in the atmosphere. People who go to bed late find it difficult to go to sleep because there is insufficient prana left for their bodies. Do not go to bed later than midnight. (25X)

If you can form the habit of going to bed early, you will be able to give your body the necessary amount of prana. If you feel tired, have an early supper and go to bed by 8 o'clock at the latest. Then you will gain more energy – which the body needs. If you have surplus energy you can go to bed later. (25X)

Sleep

Sleep is one of the most important things in the life of human beings. (25–22)

Sleep is due to the channelling of brain energy in another direction. (65X–18)

People enter into contact with the energies of living nature in their sleep and nature renovates them. (90–16)

When you go to bed you should be asleep within ten or fifteen minutes. This can be achieved only when you liberate your mind from everything you have done during the day. You should not think about your work on the following day. (95X–66)

If you are not able to sleep quietly, apply your will-power to learning how to sleep well. (95X–62)

People should improve their blood circulation if they want to sleep well. To that end one should perspire twice a week by drinking hot water. (84X–127)

Sleep is related to the astral, that is, the spiritual life of man. People learn spiritually only during their sleep. (95X–62)

It is not recommended for people who are not in harmony with each other to sleep in the same room. When people sleep, their astral bodies come out of the physical and may be subject to alien influences – that is why they should pray for the assistance of their invisible helpers. If people do not pray and cannot protect themselves, they will be imbued with the disharmonious thoughts and feelings of the other person and it will take them a long time to free themselves from the alien influence. (76X)

People should know how to sleep – I mean their position before falling asleep, so that their astral doubles may go out freely and find their Master to teach them. Spiritual knowledge is taught while people sleep, not in the physical world. While people are on earth they study, practise and apply what they have been taught in their sleep. (95X–62)

Note: the position recommended by Beinsa Douno is on the right side, with the right hand under the head and the left along the left leg. This permits a free circulation of energy; the legs should not be crossed.

People learn even in their sleep, they solve problems that have troubled them during the day. That is why one should not hurry to solve all one's problems. Go to sleep and you will have a good solution to your problem in the morning. (95X–79)

When you sleep you go to school in the astral world. What you learn at night is applied during the day. You regard sleep as rest which is why you cannot find those beings who wish to teach you. In that respect you resemble those children who run away from school. That is why, when you go to bed, say to yourself, 'Now I am going to school in the astral world to learn something new – which I shall apply on earth.' (25–23)

You need seven hours' sleep. Five hours can be enough – but only if you sleep continuously without waking up or turning from side to side. (25–29)

If people sleep after the sun is up it is like being placed under a waterfall and being struck by the water. Such is the influence of the sun's energy on the nervous system. (45–191)

PRAYER AND CONTEMPLATION

Beinsa Douno left many prayers and formulas, some of which have appeared in a privately printed booklet compiled by the present editor. The selections included here speak of the nature of prayer as a tuning to the higher world and an absorption into one's inner depths. We are also encouraged to choose a special time of day to dedicate to inner spiritual work so as to make it an integral part of our lives, a conversation with the inner, invisible world in the course of which we receive guidance and support. A deepening of our current impulse to meditate will lead us gently into prayer and a growing awareness that we do not tread the path of life alone.

> Be always faithful, true, pure and gentle,
> And the God of Peace will fill your heart with all goodness.

• • •

The greatest thing in the world is prayer. It connects us with God – the Eternal Principle within us that bestows meaning and significance. (108X)

Prayer is the great state of the soul which allows human beings to make conscious and noetic contact with the beings who have completed their development. (76X)

Prayer is tuning the consciousness to the higher worlds. Such tuning is similar to tuning the strings of a violin. (78X)

I do not refer to the kind of prayer caused by fear. That is not prayer. By the word prayer I mean a connection and communion with God. (64X)

It is said in the Scriptures: 'But when thou prayest, enter into thy closet, and when thou hast shut the door, pray to thy Father which is in secret, and the Father which seeth in secret shall reward thee openly.' The secret room is the spiritual body. This is the only way in which humans will find God, the angels and the Church. (27X)

What does secret prayer mean? It means closing the telephone lines linked with the outside world. When a person is praying within himself he has to be free; he should disconnect every line with the world; he should be deaf to every noise and every sound within and without. If you are praying secretly, switch off every key and connection with the world, so as to be free from disturbances. Then remain alone and contemplate. A secret prayer is one that raises the mind to God. In other words, a secret prayer means directing the eyes towards the sun, the source of life. The most beautiful prayer is for people to think of God as the source of life. (25X)

When you pray, you should be upright and supple. Never pray sitting down. (103X)

The most natural position for prayer is to shut your eyes and be deeply absorbed within. (21X)

If you want to teach a person how to pray, take him into an orchard to a tree laden with fruit and say: 'Lift up your arms and pick a ripe fruit.' When he raises his arms, tell him: 'This is the way a person should pray.' (45X)

If people's minds are uplifted and exalted and if they entertain sublime thoughts at a meeting – then Christ visits them for at least five or ten minutes; if Christ does not come, then it will be another representative of the White Brotherhood. It is sufficient for two people to raise their thoughts for Christ to visit them. (17X)

Each prayer and impulse of gratitude which springs from the heart is always received. God hears the slightest call and answers it. (21X)

When you look for God with a pure heart, He comes immediately and helps. (21X)

As disciples you have to maintain your link with the invisible world and draw energies from it. If you do not maintain that contact, you will soon become like reservoirs: there will be some water within you, but you will be expecting it to rain all the time to keep you full. If, however, you keep up your contact with the invisible world, you will become mountain springs that will give water all the time. Each person's task is to become a spring which gives out everything to everybody. (90X)

Now all of you should take a deep breath and concentrate – as if you have no connections with life on earth. Life on earth is a rucksack which is not so very important. Now you will put that rucksack on the floor and feel like new-born babies. After the prayer you may put one, two, three or ten rucksacks on your backs – that depends on you – but while you are praying you should have no rucksacks on your backs. You will be extraordinarily awake and free, as if you were living in heaven. What will happen tomorrow is not important and does not interest you. This day is God's day. We are interested in this day so that we may receive one of God's gifts. This day should be marked by a divine gift. (53X)

The best time for meditation is in the morning and when you are well disposed. Every person is free to choose the best time. (25X)

Every one of you who wants to be a disciple must choose a sacred hour for work. This sacred hour can be in the

morning, in the afternoon or in the evening. Spend this
hour in deep meditation in order to deal effectively with all
the difficulties encountered on your path. After such an
hour spent in meditation you should feel encouraged and
refreshed, your heart purified, so that you may spend the
rest of the day feeling invigorated. (6)

I say that you should observe this sacred hour throughout
the year and work towards the restoration of harmony in
your relations, towards the overcoming of difficulties and
towards your spiritual elevation. I give each of you the
task of ascertaining which hour of the day is your sacred
hour. There is a definite sacred hour for each disciple.
When you discover this hour, a great thought and noble
feeling will appear in your mind and heart. In general
you will experience a state of inner illumination. If you
make room for that thought and feeling within yourself
you will be uplifted, but if you oppose them you will
sense darkness in your consciousness and will have to
wait a long time until you rediscover your sacred hour.
The sacred hour comes regularly every day at the same
time. You will distinguish this hour from other hours of
the day by the fact that it is more intense and has a finer
tone. (6)

I am speaking about that conscious human life, about
conscious prayer, that ceaseless inner aspiration of the soul
towards union with God. I am not speaking about the kind
of prayer which is merely a repetition of words written by
other people. Prayer is a ceaseless aspiration of the soul
towards working with God. Then our interests become the
same as those of God. In order not to break our contact
with God, whatever we undertake to accomplish during
the day should be done with the unique thought that it is
for God. (6)

It is written in the Scriptures: 'An angel of the Lord guards
those who pray to God and rely on Him.' Therefore, when
you pray and call on God to help you, a being of light will
come from the invisible world to accompany you in the
difficult and terrible hours of your life. No person can
travel the path alone; no one can fulfil the work assigned
to them on their own. Somebody must come to their aid.

When you find yourself in a difficult situation, pray sincerely; you will immediately be assisted by some beings who help mankind. (3)

It is written in the Scriptures: 'Pray without ceasing.' This means: always be in contact with the divine world. The person who prays sincerely from the heart will certainly receive an answer to a prayer. (3)

We regard prayer as a conversation with the invisible world, a talk with God. To pray is to learn to speak. We are suffering today because we have not learned the heavenly divine language in which one's entire spirit, soul and mind participate. What a person wants of God must have a single inner meaning. When you pray, say: 'Lord, may Thy will be done. I will gladly accept all that comes from Thy hand and will fulfil Thy will without breaking Thy law.' (6)

When you find yourself in a state of great tribulation and cannot resolve some question, say: 'The will of God be done.' When you say this, the question will soon be resolved. (3)

Sacrifice always out of love and in the name of God. When you act in this way, say: 'Hallowed be the name of God. May the will of God be done! May the Kingdom of God come!' Be prepared to sacrifice yourself for the name of God, for the will of God and for the Kingdom of God. This will elevate your souls and make you citizens of the Kingdom of God. (3)

Concentration

Concentration is critical: the mind should not stray. (50–4)

Concentration means selecting good thoughts and dwelling on them. Don't think it is easy for a person to concentrate and be patient. It is one of the difficult arts. (50–9)

While unfolding their sensitivity, people need to know how to guard against negative feelings and thoughts which disturb their inner disposition. In order to transform their state, people have to concentrate deeply within themselves and find the good side of everything. When people meditate and look deeply within, they see the beauty and harmony which reign in the totality of life. This is the only way that they come to realize that all the events of their life happen for their benefit. Through contemplation people learn to control their thoughts and to concentrate in one direction. This is the significance of contemplation. (76X–119)

Controlling a thought means being able to follow its direction; to see where it is coming from and where it is going and, according to your understanding, either to let it go, transform it or stop it. (28–198)

In order to be able to deal with all the energies within yourself – positive or negative – you need to study the law of concentration. When a person is concentrated, he is able to control fear. The ability to control the passing energies means being able to use them noetically. A person studying the laws of concentration should do experiments like fixing his eyes on an object without blinking. Try this experiment – starting with one minute, then gradually increase the time. That helps to strengthen the eyes. Your consciousness has to be concentrated when you perform this experiment. Your thoughts and consciousness should not stray. (34–45)

When disciples think about a problem they should make a supreme effort in order to awaken the activity of all the brain centres or, at least, a good part of them. If only one centre is awake, the person will certainly fall asleep in a state of self-hypnosis. (28–233)

Suppose a person sits down and concentrates. What happens to the European? He thinks and thinks, finally falling asleep in the process. That is not concentration at all. What about the Indians? Those people have many systems of concentration and have used singing and playing musical instruments for centuries. They have passed the first stage of study and have arrived at concentration. (80X–8)

Nowadays people complain that they cannot realize a single idea that comes into their minds. Why is this?

Because doubts penetrate the mind. If you want to tackle your doubts, concentrate your thoughts, thus linking them with noetic higher beings who will always come to your aid. (76X–64)

HEALTH

We have already seen that the physical body is regarded as the temple of the soul and spirit, and that the will is developed on a number of levels through appropriate discipline and exercise. Beinsa Douno's integrated approach to life puts a premium on health, not simply physical well-being but an overall harmony between thoughts and feelings, between the brain, the lungs and the stomach, and between human beings and God. His lectures contained many detailed recommendations for the maintenance of health; these have been organized here under seven sub-headings.

• • •

What does health represent? Organized matter, organized energy, organized thought. (26)

A healthy person is one with mind, heart and will in complete harmony – with light in the mind, an impulse and stimulus in the heart, and energy in the will. (10)

A sound body is a well-organized one in which there are no fats, no excesses. A sound body means an absolute harmony between the cells of the brain, the lungs and the stomach – between all the organs. In such a condition a person feels joy when thinking, feeling and acting. That is the normal condition of the body. (19)

When the stomach functions well – the body is healthy; when the heart feels properly – the soul is harmonious; when the mind thinks correctly – the spirit is sound. If you wish to warm your hearts and enlighten your minds, you should restore the harmony between thoughts and feelings. (84X)

People are healthy, clever and good when they have

energy within themselves; they can then withstand the contradictions encountered in nature. (46)

To be healthy means to be in harmony with the primordial principle, with your dear ones and with yourself. (10)

Nutrition

Nutrition, defined below as 'a science concerned with the transformation of energies from one state to another', is to be understood in its widest sense. Most people simply think of food and water without considering that we can derive vital energy from air and light. The latter view underlies the practice of rising early in the spring and summer to greet the sun and absorb the early morning prana. Nutrition through breathing is treated in a separate section.

The thoughts and feeling which accompany the process of eating are extremely important. You may have observed that you do not digest so well if you are stressed or upset. Ideally, one should eat with a feeling of gratitude in one's mind and heart: gratitude for the food itself, to the tree or plant which has produced it and to those who have grown it and transported it. To feel grateful is to eat in peace and harmony, to be aware of the divine gift which food represents. It is also worth remembering the value of chewing food properly, not only because digestion and assimilation are improved, but also because the vital force of the food is partly extracted in the mouth.

The grace given by Beinsa Douno before meals is the following formula repeated three times: Bojiata Liubov noci isolbilnia i peuln jivot *(The love of God brings fullness of life). In another formula, which one can pronounce three times as a prayer, he says:*

Break the bread with love and reflect that God is within it.
Drink the water with love and reflect that God is within it.
Breathe the air with love and reflect that God is within it.
Contemplate the light with love and reflect that God is within it.

We saw above that feelings are food for the heart and thoughts food for the mind. If one is careful about one's physical diet, one should pay equal attention to one's emotional, mental and spiritual nutrition. We can absorb and process thoughts and feelings in an analagous way to food and drink; if we think that our food is polluted by biological poisons and our air by car-exhaust emissions, the same can be said about the pollution of our mental and spiritual atmospheres: hence the emphasis on purity.

•   •   •

People derive vital energies from several sources: food, air, water and light. (94X-9)

A person wishing to develop properly should first of all absorb light correctly, then heat, then air and, finally solid food for the body. (32-63)

The fundamental rules for the hygiene of good nutrition are the following: the correct absorption of light, heat, air and solid food. When the mind, heart and lungs have received their food, the body is ready to receive its food – then we can say that a person has eaten properly. (32-64)

Correct eating and thorough assimilation of food means a sound body. (32-64)

The internal, spiritual side of nutrition is appropriate feeling. There is a close link between nutrition and feeling. If the person links eating with the aspirations of the heart, the process is properly accomplished and will bring good results. We can then say that if a person eats and feels properly, he is healthy – both physically and emotionally. (32-239)

Nutrition is a science concerned with the transformation of energies from one state to another. (60X-60)

Food creates us, it is capable of elevating us but also of lowering us. (27-310)

The future of a people is determined by the food they eat. The purer and healthier the food, the greater and brighter their future. It is important for people to learn to use all the energy in a food. (64X-31)

It is impossible for people to eat meat and be absolutely healthy. (32–268)

People who eat plants live longer than those who eat meat. (83X–36)

Nature has spread a rich table before every person and every living being, but she never says what they should eat and how. Every person has to choose food for themselves. Some food is common to many but some is specific to individuals. Every person should know what food is especially suitable for them. People will suffer if they eat food that is inappropriate to them. Foods which do not correspond to particular individuals will cause disturbances in the body. (26–67)

In order to know which food is sound, you need to observe its effects upon your thoughts, feelings and actions. (27–33)

Study the influence of the various kinds of food on your body so that you know what food suits you. (97X–116)

You will come to resemble the food you eat. This law applies in both physical and mental realms. (97X–24)

If a pregnant mother does not know what and how to eat, she will not be able to have a good and peaceful child. (87X–314)

Nutrition and eating are the greatest energies condensed into such a visible shape. (70X–10)

The process of eating is a sacred act which should be approached with due reverence. (21–284)

Beginning a meal is an important matter: it makes a difference whether you start straight away or rather pause in front of the dining table, give thanks for the gift of food, say the prayer: 'The Love of God brings fullness of life,' and then begin to eat. (64X–4)

Eating is a conscious process. It has to be done consciously so that you will be able to make use of the food you have taken in. (97X–27)

If your mind is not concentrated while eating, it is a waste of time. (36–183)

If your eating is not accompanied by an inner feeling, the process is not being properly carried out. (32–339)

While you are eating, you should not allow a single bad thought to enter your mind or a single bad feeling to penetrate your heart. (64X–73)

The mind, heart and will should all take part in the process of eating. Only in this way can a person be healthy and retain a youthful vigour. (84X–121)

Food should remain longer in the mouth so that part of its energy can penetrate the tongue. The tongue extracts the spiritual energy from the food which cannot otherwise be absorbed (87X–3)

People who chew their food well do not fall ill. If you chew your food only on the right or the left side, you cannot be healthy. (89X–32)

You cannot avail yourselves of the energy of food you do not like. (89X–57)

There should be a relation between you and the food you eat. Eat food which suits you and talk to it. This means that you should use living, not dead, food. Dead food is of no use to anyone. (97X–202)

What is the most important thing when you are eating? To eat with gratitude and contentment. If you can remain contented among discontented people and influence them, you are a genius. The contented person brings music into the meal. You must be the first to show your contentment – then the others will follow. (38–60)

One of the most important rules for eating is never to eat a lot. You should always feel a little hungry. That should be your ideal. If you leave the table completely full, you have not observed the divine law. Let your stomach be one third empty. (89X–14)

After every meal you have to transform what you have eaten into a feeling – a sublime feeling. That is the treasure; that is the growth of the heart. We should not stop there. That energy has to be sent to our minds and it has to create the highest, the most sublime thoughts. Then the soul grows properly and those functions gradually build our body. (40–9)

Fasting

Naturopathic medicine has always recommended fasting as a way of purification and renovation of the physical organism. It will be seen from the selections that there is a physical level of fasting and a spiritual level, both of which involve a filtering process and a burning up of poisons and negativity. Disciples in Bulgaria most commonly fast between Thursday and Friday lunchtime when they eat 'Angel's Soup'. I do not have the exact recipe but know it contains potatoes, carrots and parsley!

● ● ●

Fasting is necessary for the body – both externally and internally. (89X–158)

Fasting lengthens our lives. (21–187)

Fasting is a way of renovating the human organism. The chief idea of fasting is to collect the hidden energies in the cells and to renovate our bodies. (17–21)

Fasting is a means of getting rid of fear, controlling the digestive system, the blood circulation and the mind. (17–22)

If for a few days you have no appetite, don't eat; wait until your desire to eat arises naturally. There are animals that do not eat when they are unwell.

Go in for fasting gradually. If you fix on a fast without knowing why you are doing it, it is not useful.

You should keep to the days you have decided to fast. If you start fasting on a Monday, the results will be of one kind; if you start on a Tuesday, the results will be different; likewise if you start on any other day of the week – the results all differ. Results will also vary according to whether you start fasting in the morning, at noon, or in the evening. (17–21)

All of you should fix one day a month for a rest – you will not eat on that day. You will rest in the physical domain but you will work in the spiritual world. That day will be the third Friday of the month; this means that you will have such a rest twelve times a year. The fasting will begin on Thursday after lunch and will end on Friday at midday. You will eat a little, both on Thursday and Friday. That to me is just a rest, not fasting. (5–106)

If you have eaten a lot, you should begin to fast. There are two kinds of fasting: physical and spiritual. (89X–194)

The purpose of fasting is to strain and filter our thoughts and feelings. To fast means to concentrate deeply within oneself and be rid of all worries and cares. (89X–194)

Fasting is recommended as a means of medical treatment. During the time of fasting the metabolism of the body is stronger; this causes all substances leading to illnesses, indisposition and dissatisfaction to be burnt up. (89X–194)

Water

Beinsa Douno set great store by the drinking of hot water (topla voda in Bulgarian) and recommended that we start the day with a mug of hot water to which one can add a slice of lemon. The primary effect of this practice is to purify the system and, if repeated often enough, to provoke sweating which brings about further purification. He treated many and diverse illnesses in his disciples through making them drink hot water and was particularly insistent about the benefits of drinking hot water in the mountains during summer camps. Up there the water is especially pure and rich in minerals as well as vital energy. There is almost always a kettle on the boil and one of the principal tasks of those on duty is to ensure a plentiful supply of water from a neighbouring spring.

•   •   •

Water contains a magical power. There is no culture
at all without water. How should one drink water?
How many glasses should one have a day? These are very
significant questions – but very few people have asked
them. (84X–122)

The first lesson is to learn how to drink water correctly
so that you link yourself with its magnetic energies.
(81X–122)

Every body requires a certain amount of water which must
be retained in the cells in order to maintain its moisture
level. If the body loses its moisture it may become dry.
Such people are usually restless and irritable. A person
who wishes to remain healthy should keep up the level of
moisture in the body. Without this inner moisture and
outer water, a person is unable to purify the body of
external and internal toxic accumulations. If these poisons
remain in the system, they will lead to unwanted illnesses.
(84X–122)

People know precious little about water – that it cleans
the body, dissolves accumulated toxins and is a good
conductor of magnetism. (84X–122)

Nature has put billions of windows in the human body –
the pores. Vital energy penetrates through them and
constantly renovates the body. These windows should
always be clean and open – so that there is a regular
exchange of internal and external air. If the windows
become dirty and various deposits build up in the pores,
the body is already exposed to various indispositions.
How will light and air enter your house if the windows
are dirty and closed? How will water enter if the pores are
blocked? (84X–122)

So the first task of the disciple is to open the pores of the
body. The pores are opened by water which provokes
sweating. (84X)

You should drink water with an awakened consciousness
so that every sip goes not only to the stomach but also to
parts of the body which are ill. (26–69)

Clean hot water helps the blood get rid of accumulated lactic and uric acid. (84X–127)

Constipation is due to lack of water in the blood. (26–89)

If you want to be healthy, you should keep in mind the beneficial action of water on the body. Drink water consciously and do not dwell on illnesses. Keep in mind thoughts of your health. Think of the beautiful and great in life and do not be afraid of anything. (84X–123)

Breathing

The connection between meditative practice and breathing techniques has a long history. We have already seen how correct breathing is a subtle form of nutrition. The main recommendation about breathing given by Beinsa Douno is that we should breathe deeply, slowly and rhythmically, an exercise which tends to calm the thoughts and feelings. Although one of the selections below suggests that he gave no breathing exercises, he did in fact give quite a number. Some are intimately linked to the paneurhythmy and others to the six or twenty-two exercises performed before the paneurhythmy, some of which are accompanied by spiritual formulas. In general, when one is breathing consciously, Beinsa Douno suggests that one thinks of life when breathing in, strength when one holds one's breath, and health when one breathes out again. Another general exercise is to breathe consciously with love, in full appreciation of the life-giving properties of the air.

Some simple exercises can be performed early in the morning or before meals. Starting with one's hands at the sides, one can raise them gradually in an arc so that they meet over the head; meanwhile, inhale. Hold for a few seconds at the top, then bring the arms back down and round to regain their starting position, gradually exhaling. A variant of this exercise is to bring one's arms straight up to the front until the hands are vertical and facing forwards; meanwhile, inhale and then hold at the top. Exhale and bring the arms down again the same way. These two exercises can be combined by bringing the arms straight up in front and then down to the sides. If performed slowly and deliberately in sequences of six, these exercises can instil great calm in mind and heart.

• • •

Living on the earth means that human beings need air as the food of their etheric and astral bodies. You are full of energy when you absorb air in the right way. Increasing levels of energy mean that people are nourishing themselves properly on air. The air contains a special energy which the Indians call *prana*. Others call it vital electricity or vital magnetism. You come to the mountains not only to breathe pure air, as many people think. You have also come to obtain some *prana*, that is, the vital power of electricity and magnetism.

You get up early in the morning in order to be able to receive the special light rays of the sun as a nourishment for your mind and its rays of warmth for the nourishment of your heart. The lungs are best at absorbing prana in the morning. (32–64)

There is a great noetic law that regulates the breathing of all living beings on the earth. (27–227)

Now when I talk about deep breathing I do not intend to recommend any special exercises. Indian people have special breathing exercises which are not appropriate to Europeans. Breathe deeply and rhythmically. When you first breathe deeply, you will become aware of a hindrance, but persistence will get rid of this and you will then acquire a freedom in your breathing. Your breathing will be complete if you open the pores of your body. This is achieved by using water. Complete breathing is not only through the lungs, but through the skin of the body. (84X–124)

The skin should be kept in a soft state since the soul breathes through it in the physical world. (82X–90)

Every cell in the human body must breathe. The person who breathes in this way can be called healthy. (84X–124)

Spend five or ten minutes simply breathing and do not think of anything else in the meantime. (28–291)

Do the exercise calmly and with concentration – so that you may achieve some results. Otherwise you will make it mechanical and achieve nothing. (23–291)

Almost everyone breathes badly. They take in air and send it to the upper part of the lungs. In their shallow and weak breathing carbon dioxide remains in the lungs and creates deposits. If people want to regulate their blood circulation, they should breathe in deeply, retain the air in their lungs for a while and then exhale very slowly. The abdominal muscles must participate in breathing. They have to create pressure to exhale the air. When a person breathes properly he renews himself and is freed from physical and psychic indispositions. (76X–131)

Love is the first precondition of complete breathing. When breathing, people should appreciate the air as an irreplaceable benefit. People who love expand their lungs. When a person receives a benefit consciously, with gratitude, love begins to operate within him and raises him. Every divine energy which descends has first to pass through the respiratory system, then it ascends to the mind and thence down to the heart. (29–134)

The air is a carrier of divine thoughts which first pass through the respiratory system where they are elaborated and transformed. From there they are carried by the blood to the brain. (12–283)

Breathing is linked with the mind, while the mind is linked with the spirit. A person who links his breathing with the aspirations of the mind will obtain beneficial results. (32–340)

The inner, spiritual side of breathing is correct thinking. (32–339)

If breathing is not accompanied by an inner thought, the process is not being carried out correctly. (32–339)

Every inhalation has to regulate and cleanse the desires, while every exhalation is linked with the purification of human thoughts. Knowing this, you should inhale and exhale consciously. This is the only way in which you can

cleanse your thoughts and desires. The lungs represent
a filter which purifies human mental and emotional life.
That filter allows through only thoughts and desires which
have not passed through another person's filter. People
need to receive new thoughts, feelings and desires every
moment so that the filter may remain active. It is
dangerous for the sift to stop working – poisons will then
accumulate which impede the correct circulation of the
blood. (46–24)

Some people are nervous and short-tempered. Why? They
do not breathe properly. (32–65)

People who are ill are recommended to breathe a lot of air
and eat only a little food. (32–63)

When spring approaches, start going out for walks every
morning, the earlier the better. Get out of the big cities, far
away from the dust and noise if possible, and breathe
deeply. You may also do some exercises for an hour. Then
you may start your day's work. If you go for a walk your
work will be easier – much easier than if you stay in your
rooms and work. (84X–124)

If you have a free half-hour, use it to breathe deeply.
Direct your thoughts upwards towards God and try to link
yourselves with Him. Breathe rhythmically. Make use of
fresh air and fresh water. (84X–124)

Purity

*'Blessed are the pure in heart, for they shall see God.' Purity
of heart corresponds to brightness and clarity of mind, a state
in which there is no impediment to perception. Beinsa Douno
gave many lectures on the theme of purity and exemplified it
in his life. One of his most beautiful formulas is this: 'May my
thoughts be as radiant as the sun and my feelings as pure as
the water from mountain springs.' We have already noted how
fasting and the drinking of water exert a purifying influence.
Here the concept is extended to include purity of thought and
feeling. It is arresting to read that gossip and criticism of other
people's defects are a form of impurity and contamination, but*

it does enable one to appreciate the scope and importance of the idea.

• • •

Without cleanliness – personal or social – there can be no development. Cleanliness is the first essential precondition for correct human development. (45–206)

An absolute cleanliness and purity is necessary for the body, for the heart and for the mind. (45–98)

Protect your body through cleanliness; it is an expression of a perfect life. (102X–3)

If you want to be healthy, work on your body so as to rid yourself of all impurities and surpluses, toxins and fats. If you notice an accumulation of fats in some part of your body you should immediately apply a spartan regime. (84X–125)

The divine will visit us when we are absolutely pure, so that it will not meet any resistance. (39–69)

By the word cleanliness I do not mean external, physical cleanliness, but rather that every cell in your body should be internally and externally clean. That general cleanliness of the cells is the cleanliness of the entire body. (53)

Everything is clean and pure until some mixtures and external elements are added to it. (3–18)

When the element of impurity begins to enter your lives, death immediately takes a step forward. (3–18)

The first regulation of life is for people to purify their thoughts. (3–18)

In order that we may live well, we should purify our flesh, making it of pure and refined matter so as to be able to receive luminous and sublime thoughts. (85X–156)

Bad thoughts and feelings give rise to very great impurities in the mental and astral worlds, greater than the impurities they cause in the physical world. (45–207)

Gossiping about other people is a form of impurity; envy and a number of other vices are impurities. (3–18)

Dwelling on the defects of other people is a kind of contamination which ruins the body. (3-18)

People should free their consciousness from all impure images. They should create within themselves pure concepts and pure images. As regards young women and young men, for instance, they should have pure images of marriage, celibacy, love, eternal life and children. (3-26)

Suffering in the world arises from the fact that the body, the heart or the mind of a person is impure. Then the divine energies entering in meet certain resistances. (39-35)

If you want to be healthy, your body has to be clean; if you want to be happy, your heart has to be clean; if you want to be a poet, to have luminous ideas, your mind must be pure. (39-36)

If you want other people to love you, you must maintain an absolute purity – because the invisible world is very exacting. (83X-80)

It is your own responsibility to maintain an absolute purity throughout your lives. If you want to be healthy and cheerful, let your every feeling, every thought and every action be permeated with purity. Only in this way will you receive the blessing of God. (3-18)

The person who takes purity as a starting point has already taken a step forward. (3-24)

Many possibilities are opened up to the pure person: progress, light, knowledge, power and freedom in the physical world depend on purity. (3-26)

Do you want to understand God? Then you have to be pure. (3-18)

The first necessary step in acquiring the divine life is purity. (3-26)

Every one of you should be distinguished by a strong striving towards purity. Purity is the first rung on the ladder of the divine Life. When you climb up to the second rung, you will read 'purity' once again. (3-26)

To acquire and retain beauty in oneself, one has to be absolutely pure. (25–100)

We must all be physically, emotionally and mentally pure. When a person's body is clean, he will be physically healthy; when his heart is pure, he will have a pleasant face and bright eyes; when his mind is pure, his face radiates a harmonious soft light. (45–20)

Cleansing

This section summarizes some of the advice given in previous selections by stressing the need for purification and the genesis of illness in residual toxins accumulating in the body.

•   •   •

It is written in the Scriptures: 'You must repent, you need cleansing!'
There are surplus elements not only in people's stomachs and hearts; in their minds and wills as well there are many unnecessary things. They all have to be thrown out. (13–16)

You should look after your health before you fall ill. (39–128)

All the pores of your body have to be opened. A person has seven million pores in the skin, that is, seven million windows which have to be open. A person can be healthy when all the pores are open. Therefore the first treatment in any disease is to open the pores of the skin – for which sweating and washing of the body is required. The sweating is best done by drinking boiling water – it comes out through the pores of the skin; in this way it opens them and restores the healthy state of the body. (82X–90)

The cause of illnesses lies in the pores being blocked. The place where the pores are blocked is the site of the illness. The body does not tolerate any impurities, any alien substances in itself. If such impurities accumulate at a certain place, then the body falls ill. Every illness is a liberation of the body from alien substances. If there is any blockage in the channels of the spinal column, people lose their vitality. The spinal cord has the capacity to absorb the *prana* or vital energy from the air and spread it through the whole body. Every blockage disturbs the regular current of the blood circulation. When the blood circulation is not regular, the body is exposed to various illnesses. (84X–125)

People should induce sweating by drinking hot water. You will have to drink several cups of hot water in which you can put a few drops of lemon juice. When you perspire profusely rub your body with a wet towel and put on clean clothes. Then you should drink another half or whole cup of hot water. (84X–127)

Dissatisfaction is a spiritual impurity which blocks the pores of the body. Get rid of it as the water cleans your bodies – open all seven million pores through which you breathe. Clean out the spiritual dirt as well so that your hearts, minds and souls may breathe freely. If a person begins to breathe in this way, his dissatisfaction will turn to satisfaction. (26–46)

Movement

Beinsa Douno encourages us to be conscious of our movements and to make them as graceful and harmonious as possible. This applies to gestures as well as the way we walk. We all know that gestures are expressive but they remain unconscious more often than not. The science of gestures was developed by Beinsa Douno into systematic exercises and, finally, into the paneu-rhythmy itself, about which I have written in another volume. Few people are aware of the polarization of the limbs by which the left hand is receptive and the right emissive. This means that one can transmit certain feelings and thoughts through gestures. To take a simple example, one can give out love and light through a gesture of the right hand, corresponding to the ecclesiastical blessing. As we become more conscious of our movements, so we are able to strengthen our wills and become more effective and harmonious.

•   •   •

Life is movement. (43-126)

When a person changes state, there is movement within. (16-25)

Movement is the result of will-power. (31-81)

What do the movements of a person represent? They represent an expenditure of energy. Every movement – conscious or unconscious – is a function of some process. People receive or give part of their energy through movement. People should make their gestures conscious and should apply them in their physical life as methods of transforming energy. Your mood can be improved through conscious and noetic gestures. (76X-84)

Natural and free gestures confer beauty on the body. Forced and unnatural gestures make people tired. (33-40)

A disharmonious movement of the mouth is capable of destroying relations with your friends. There are movements of sin and crime, which a person can perform with his eyes, nose and eyebrows, causing disharmony in his whole life. (27-206)

Disharmonious movements disturb the body in the same way as bad and putrified food. (22-130)

Gestures should always be conscious and thoughtful, in accordance with certain noetic laws. (56-98)

You must perform movements that are pleasant, with which you yourselves are pleased. When you perform a natural movement in accordance with the laws of nature, you will feel a great inner pleasure.
   When you perform an unnatural gesture, you will feel that someone has cut you with a knife. (83X-175)

Every physical movement is accompanied by an inner change. (76X-92)

A movement is noetic when it is in harmony with the movements of all noetic beings. When all beings are in harmony with us, we feel an inner joy. (65X-59)

The movements of a person demonstrate whether he will

be linked to the ascending or descending currents of nature. (76X–92)

A person who raises an arm upwards is calling for help from the noetic energies of nature. (76X–148)

When you raise your arm you are linked with the divine world – with the noetic beings of light. (71X–80)

If you wish to receive the energies of the sun, you should do your exercises in the morning. If you wish to rid yourselves of the energy collected during the day, you should do your exercises in the evening. (21–126)

Every movement we make, every thought, every feeling should be in harmony with the whole divine law of all beings which are within that collective consciousness. (65X–50)

The essential feature of human harmony is that everything should be plastic, flexible and dynamic, thus unbreakable. Static things are fragile and breakable. (38–83)

The person who understands the language of movements can read them, studying others and himself. (22–120)

People can be known by the way in which they walk. (22–23)

Everything a person thinks or feels is reflected in the walk. (22–23)

You should walk uprightly – not like a soldier, but like a poet or philosopher, the thoughts of whom are concentrated on what they are doing. There must be rhythm in your walk: start slowly and then speed up. (22–100)

If you learn first to step on the toes and then the heels, you will avoid jarring your spine. (76X–52)

When a person sets out for somewhere, he will first turn to God and put his right foot forward – then he will start walking. The mind should be first, followed by the heart. (22–28)

If you are calling someone to go somewhere, they should not hurry; they should stop, think awhile, pray inwardly and prepare to go. We do not achieve anything if we hurry. (22–28)

When you walk your movements should be in harmony with your general thoughts and feelings. (83X–175)

When you meet someone who finds that life is worth living, you will see that he is walking courageously with his head up; his steps are sure. (22–28)

The good person walks quietly – like water. (22–28)

The person who lives harmoniously walks in a musical way. There is plasticity and pliability. (54–162)

WORK

The everyday conception of work is to divide it into mental or physical categories, brain work or manual work. These ideas do not usually go as far as inner work, work on oneself, on one's mind and heart. This kind of work is associated with spiritual disciplines by which one attempts to refine and purify one's thoughts and feelings. Beinsa Douno recommends that we spend time on spiritual, mental, emotional and physical work, along similar lines to the Benedictine Rule which prescribes specific hours for different kinds of activity. Just as trees and plants work to produce flowers and fruit, so human beings can work to cultivate the divine seeds and talents implanted within them. This is the most significant form of human creation for, in the higher realms, to work is to create and to create is to work.

Throughout his teaching, Beinsa Douno emphasized the importance of having a high ideal in mind when one is working. The ideal brings coherence and direction into our actions, leading to a concentration of efforts. One such ideal is to devote one's work to the coming of the Kingdom of God on earth and to do everything for the glory of God. The following formulas express this sentiment:

May we all have an ideal which prevents us from going astray; may we always seek to serve the divine and better to express love in its innumerable forms.

May we be studious, working with a pure heart and a radiant mind. May love be the basis of all our deeds.

> *May there be sweetness in our words,*
> *Truth in our look,*
> *Justice in our decisions,*
> *Kindness in our actions.*

> *May we be as pure as light,*
> *As transparent as water,*
> *As abundant as love,*
> *As luminous as truth,*
> *As harmonious as wisdom,*
> *As firm and unshakeable as justice,*
> *As stable as virtue.*

Lord, I thank Thee for giving me a good mind in which Thou hast implanted Thy wisdom, a good heart in which Thou hast implanted Thy love. With this love and wisdom I wish to accomplish Thy will.

• • •

Coming to earth means that people have a certain mission to fulfil. To this end they are given a certain capital which has to be put into the work and added to. (76X–37)

To avail yourselves of the benefits of life, you have to have worked to gain them. (89X–238)

As disciples you have to maintain a constant impulse to work. Through work and exercise you develop the strength of your body. Nature loves strong and bold people because they can use her goods. (116X)

The essential thing that contemporary people need to do is conscious work. In this way they will find the talents that nature has invested in them. That kind of work is inner and spritual. (46–211)

You have to work to develop your talents which can be achieved only when you are in harmony with noetic nature. (46–211)

Correcting some of your faults or acquiring good qualities is work. It is noble work to want to become generous, brave and prudent. (83X)

All work is important according to the law of divine wisdom to which love and truth are attendants. All work – however microscopic – is sacred. (78X–50)

The motive of your work has to be in harmony and agreement with God, the Great Principle in the world. That means noetic work. (76X–216)

Begin to work conscientiously, limiting and not torturing yourself. Rid yourself of everything that impedes you in life. Work for what you lack. (25–40)

When you are in doubt about something, do not try to realize it. (18–51)

You need to map out your work in such a way that you will work part of it for yourself, part for your dear ones, and part for God. In other words you will use a part of your time for your mind, part of it for your heart, and part for your body. (45–99)

The strong person does not know vexation. He performs his work calmly, quietly and with a great pleasure. (103X–67)

When you start some work and your spirit is not at ease, that does not show that you cannot finish that work, but rather that the method you have chosen is not correct. (103X–68)

Prayers by themselves do not resolve hardships. You will pray, you will think and you will work until you resolve the hardship. (46–280)

Even if you make a hundred mistakes, do not give up your work. (38–6)

A person makes an effort and contributes towards the solution of a given problem. The person who fails to understand this thinks that he is solving the problem alone. Nobody is working alone. Many invisible noetic beings are helping people. (4–35)

It is recommended that people work in three directions: a few hours on the mind, an hour or two on the heart and two to four on the body – physical work. (95X–234)

Normal people do everything with pleasure. They never overburden themselves with surplus work. They undertake only what they can accomplish. They do everything in accordance with the law of freedom. (18–188)

People should work hard but not inordinately so. There should be no surfeit in your work. People should work as long as they feel pleasure. True work is that which organizes human energies. (90X–302)

The disciple should not give up the work he has done until he achieves a result. (28–61)

Every person has been given some work that they alone have to finish. If they do not complete the work which God demands, they cannot be free. They will have to return to earth thousands of times until they carry out the work required by God. (45–214)

Every work accomplished with love and tranquillity brings a blessing to the person. (2–247)

To serve God, to feel a connection and always to be ready to perform the divine action – therein lie the energy, wealth, power and knowledge of human beings. (78–78)

The person who is content and industrious is polishing himself and begins to shine. (32–77)

Be 'Sons of Light'! The conception 'Sons of Light' means those noetic beings who have come to the earth to work, create and build – not to eat and drink. They are people both of the pen and the hammer at the same time. If you go into the fields, you will find them there. They plough, dig, build and construct. They are good workers in every direction. Whatever passes through their hands comes to life and revives. (27–107)

Work lovingly and consciously so that people will one day say of you: 'There is a person created in the image and likeness of God.' (27–43)

People should solve this important question every day: why have they come to earth and what work do they have to do? Let each individual ask himself what task and what work has been given to him. (9–91)

In what way can we fulfil our mission, our destiny on earth? I say: Let everybody remain in their place and serve God where they are. The various posts you occupy are conditions and elements necessary for the achievement of your tasks. (39–100)

The great task for human beings is to work and study – beginning from small units and proceeding to larger ones. (56–197)

The task of the disciple is to govern the mind and heart, that is, his thoughts, feelings and capacities. These have to be under the control of the noetic will. (95X–113)

The first task of human beings is not in turning people to God, but rather in working on themselves. (56–205)

The task of every person is to realize that idea which has been planted in the soul. They should understand that they have to remain loyal to their ideal in all circumstances. (27–301)

Your present task is to correct your past faults. If you cannot correct the mistakes of the past, you will not be able to make use of the new conditions. (11)

There is no question of people making piecemeal improvements to their lives – they will have to overhaul them completely. People all have sublime ideas. All of you have to accept love as a law. Every person should know his place and stage of development – so that he may unfold further. (97X–193)

People are determined by their aspirations. Our true nature is only what aims at the Primary Principle. Only that is unchangeable. All other phenomena, constantly changing as they are, represent means and training aids to be used. (46–174)

Do not fear character-forming hardships and suffering.

They give us direction and purpose in our lives.
(46–240)

The aim of life is that people should realize immortality on earth – something that will remain eternally. (56–225)

VIRTUES

We work inwardly in order to unfold and develop our virtues and talents, to reveal the image of the divine within us. The conditions of life are the soil in which our virtues can grow. Saint Paul wrote eloquently about the fruits of the spirit, fruits which are perennial and need to grow anew on the trees of every fresh generation. The most sublime quality is love, which Beinsa Douno relates to peace, and from peace to joy, defined as the inner flow of love, a springtime blossom in the soul. None of these qualities can be realized without the faith which provides the connecting link with the divine world. Faith excludes doubt and promotes courage in facing the inevitable storms of life. On retiring to bed, the following formula is recommended: 'The faith in which I live instils divine harmony into the aspirations of my heart.' If faith is the first wing of love, hope is the second. Hope is the essential antidote to despair, a connection more evident in French with the two words espoir and désespoir. It is hope that sustains us through the trials of the physical world, but not without its companion principles of faith and love. Beinsa Douno explained these three principles and their connections in some depth in a number of lectures, always coming back to the essentials which are the prerequisite of an abundant and creative existence.

> *Have unshakeable faith: 'Such is the will of God, who is pure love and wisdom; everything is for the best.' Such an attitude resolves all difficulties, enabling a negative situation to be transformed into a positive one, leading to strength of soul, freedom in thought and the faculty of constant self-perfection.*

• • •

When love descends to the physical world, it turns into virtue. (39–107)

The true person should be like gold, both externally and internally. (50–206)

Where does a person's greatness lie? In the virtues they have developed. (27–280)

What is life? It is the art of acquiring virtues and knowing how to decorate ourselves with them. (111X–247)

The true virtues come from within, while the conditions for their development are external. Life is the first condition for the unfolding of virtues. (27–327)

You should all work consciously to unfold the virtues and talents invested within you. It is written in the Scriptures that you are the likeness of God. How can you realize this? By persistent, conscious work on yourself. That is the great task given to every person, not simply in the course of a year or even a lifetime – but throughout the ages. That means during your whole time on earth. (37–93)

The realization of a virtue is linked with great hardships. Every virtue represents an organism that gradually grows and develops. To give birth to a virtue, that is, to manifest it, shows the correct link between the human soul and God. The link between the thoughts, the feelings and the actions of a person is also correct. (34–99)

If you use your talents only for your own ends, you will lose them. If you want to keep them, you will have to work with them not only for your own benefit but also for the benefit of your dear ones. (58X–273)

The fruits of the spirit are love, peace, endurance, kindness, mercy, faith, meekness, self-restraint. Love is the father, joy is the mother, peace is their child. The people who wish to be blessed should possess these fruits. (31–73)

There are virtues that belong to the angelic world: long-sufferingness is the father, mildness the mother and mercy their child. If you acquire these virtues you will be among the angels. (31–13)

The third category: faith the father, meekness the mother, self-restraint their child. (31–13)

You need first of all to master your feelings because they are in your hands and at your disposal. You will then learn to master your tongue, your eyes, your nose and your ears. (13–21)

A good person is one who never becomes turbid or besmirched. A good person never loses purity. Is it possible to muddy the water of a deep mountain lake? A good person never takes offence. (32–73)

Beauty is a spiritual quality. Beauty is an expression of truth. Beauty is an expression of sensitivity. If you wish to be good-looking, work with your sensitivity. (22–191)

Love unfolds mercy and mercy makes people warm-hearted, sympathetic and understanding with respect to the weaknesses of others. (28–200)

To be good, people need to display mildness. The latter is determined by two qualities: kind-heartedness and sensitivity. (18–182)

To be young means throwing away every unnecessary burden and keeping only the essential. (28–11)

If a person is well-disposed towards all living beings: flowers, birds, mammals, people – he is unusual, he loves all beings and treats them all well. (27–196)

You should aspire to be an example of purity. You should have radiant thoughts, sublime feelings and perform noble actions – examples not in words but in deeds; examples in everything. (28)

People have to work out and apply the ideas they accept. If they accept ideas without applying them, they accumulate deposits in their systems which cause illness. (90–23)

Without joy there could be neither light nor warmth. (57–170)

Some people say: 'I have no peace in my life.' You
have no peace because you have no love within you.
(14–24)

Peace brings an inner silence. (109X–390)

Some people pray to God saying: 'Lord, bring peace to my
soul.' Such people turn to God as to a being outside
themselves. People should first know that God is within
them. God lies deeply hidden in their souls. If God is
within us, this peace should be there as well. Why do
people look for peace from outside? Peace is a divine, not
a human, quality. Therefore, the more we allow God to
manifest within us, the greater our possibilities of attaining
peace. (56–200)

When something great is about to come to the world, one
of the symptons is a motionless inner calm. That is called
peace. (109X–390)

When a person reaches the silence of eternal peace, all
current problems will be resolved. (14–78)

Every person who has acquired unity within has a
profound inner peace and balance. (14–63)

Joy comes after peace. (104X–390)

Joy is an inner flow of the love that has arisen. It is
preceded by peace. (109X–380)

Contemporary people miss out on joy. Every person has a
worm within himself which gnaws away at the heart.
(14–130)

No, do not leave anything bad inside your heart! When I
wake up in the morning I see how people impede
themselves. If you are not feeling well, say to yourself:
'God is well pleased, all the worlds and all the angels are
joyful. Then why should I impede myself?' (109X–187)

Everybody emerging from the tunnel to meet the first ray
of the sun feels a great joy that they have come out of the
valley of their lives. Every person should feel that joy.
(14–137)

Joy shows that life is beginning to blossom. That blossoming takes place in human consciousness. (109X–330)

Faith is a rope which you hold in this world and in the next. (89X–261)

Faith has a divine origin, belief a human one. (89X–201)

Faith – as an inner stimulus of the mind – leads people to the field of knowledge. People do not know that area, but there is a certain link between the human mind and the noetic faculty. (57–90)

We are talking of that kind of faith which is the result of knowledge. For instance, people believe that spring will return because of their knowledge of previous years. (27–151)

When faith grows stronger without the acquisition of knowledge, it is superstition. (97X–90)

Faith has raised many ill and dying people from their beds. Everyone can trust the power of faith. It is a spark that can ignite a huge fire. (27–408)

For a person to believe in something they have not tried means to live in darkness. To believe in something one has tried means to live in the light. (26–196)

People are calm when they have an absolute faith in God. When they have such a faith, it is sufficient just to think of God for their minds immediately to be filled with radiant thoughts. (17)

Faith and love are two noetic powers which operate by opposite methods and scales. Faith operates on a large scale, and love in a small way. When you find yourself facing large challenges, you will use the sign of faith. When you have small hardships, you will use the sign of love. Faith overcomes the great hardships and love the small ones. People's lack of success in life is due to inconsistency of method. (76X–46)

The divine creed requires a faith grounded in love. (14–196)

When we love God, we have an absolute faith. (14–146)

8

Relations with Nature

We are living at a time when people are beginning to rediscover nature as living and sacred. Books written ten years ago spoke of the death of nature, while now we are seeing titles on the rebirth of nature. It is not nature which changes, however, but our ideas and interpretations. For 300 years we have been in the grip of a mechanistic world-view which encouraged us to see the whole of creation as a grand clockwork mechanism and ourselves as biochemical computers. This understanding is giving way to the scientific picture of Gaia as a self-regulating organism and the correspondingly popular view of the earth as alive.

Beinsa Douno went further than this: for him nature was not simply alive but also intelligent. What we see is only the end product of work performed by noetic beings which underlies visible processes. I have discussed this at greater length in The Circle of Sacred Dance. For our purposes here, however, it is sufficient to note that nature is alive and intelligent and to mention some of the ways by which we may enter into contact with these living intelligences.

It goes without saying that one can only enter into conscious contact with an intelligence which one recognizes. A philosophy of nature which treats the world as an inanimate mechanism precludes such a possibility. In Beinsa Douno's school he encouraged the disciples to practise various forms of exchange with nature: nutrition, in which one consciously assimilates the energy of the food; attending sunrise, where the early morning prana can be absorbed; spending time in the mountains, the home of sublime beings whose presence can be sensed in the ancient sacred places said to have been frequented by Orpheus; drinking mountain water and breathing mountain air; and finally, in the practice of paneurhythmy itself, defined as a conscious noetic exchange with the intelligence of nature. Many of the gestures comprise both giving and receiving. The integration of nature and health into the teaching of Beinsa Douno makes it one of the first genuine eco-spiritual traditions.

The following invocation can be used in any open space. Looking at the sky, the sun, the clouds, the trees, the flowers, the grass, let us feel the grandeur of God; let us be filled with veneration towards Him for the beauty of nature, and let us make this invocation with our whole heart and soul:

> *Great art Thou, O Lord!*
> *Great are Thy works!*
> *Great is Thy name above all things!*
> *I send Thee my love!*
> *I see Thee and love Thee in and within the whole creation!*
> *I shall serve Thee throughout all eternity.*

•   •   •

Nature is great not only in its structure but in the intelligence and sensitivity which it manifests. We are all today under the direct guidance, not of God but of nature. (108X)

Nature is alive. (67X)

Living nature is nothing other than an aggregation of the activities of countless noetic beings. (45X)

You know that all things in nature are alive, so you have to be very respectful towards everything. If you have such wisdom, you will look at a plant and then look up to the sky every time you pass one: this out of respect for the life which manifests itself in this plant. It is a small form which is an image of the thought of God. (6)

Divine thought manifests itself everywhere. It transforms and regulates all things, so that when we refer to living nature we mean the manifestation of divine thought, the manifestation of that great law through which God works in the world. (6)

What does noetic nature represent? A life fashioned in three modes: a physical side which holds conditions and possibilities within itself; a spiritual side which comprises all laws, and a mental or divine side which includes all facts and principles that operate in the whole of life; finally, and above all, the great noetic order which directs the conditions and possibilities, as well as the laws, the facts and the principles. (27X)

The language of nature is common to all beings. It is similar to Esperanto. All the angels speak it. The person wishing to comprehend the significance of life should definitely know that language. (15)

The person who finds a place in nature and who understands his destiny will be able to fulfil his function as a limb of the great divine organism. (18)

Be in harmony with noetic nature which has foreseen all your needs and satisfies them. There is no power in the world which is capable of diverting a person from the path that noetic nature has drawn up. (46X)

You have to overcome the difficulties and challenges of life. You should be in harmony with God and work according to the laws of living nature. (26)

To human beings nature is simply a possibility of manifesting their potential and building their characters. Nature represents the objective divine world from which we have to form our internal subjective world. Everything we see outside is divine and real. First, we have to accept it within ourselves. Then we have to project it outwards so as to create our objective world. This is the only way in which people can create their own characters. God comes to help human beings. He works on separate individuals and the whole of mankind at the same time. (95X)

Everything in nature has its place. Flowers, mountain springs and stones represent letters which everybody can read. (26X)

If you go up to a river and watch its current, you will be in a pleasant mood when you leave. (80X)

You will be inspired in nature when you are out in it. This is an art in itself! You will listen to hear how the mountain spring sings. What pleasant music there is among the small stones! In some places in the forest when the leaves of the trees are whispering, there is a special music! To understand the voices of the animals and birds – especially when they begin to sing – what a concert that is! One hears how the birds begin their prayer. (16X)

When you enter into the vastness of nature, think of the air, of the light, of the mountain springs, of the stars, but never think of yourself. If you think of yourself, you will not be able to develop properly. (85X)

Nature has an abundance of vital energy, especially in April and May. Every day in those months is worth a fortune. What people can acquire in those months is unobtainable at any other time. No chemist's shop in the world can give people what nature has in store for them. If people know how to use the energies of nature, they will obtain so much energy in just one month that they will emanate a vigorous and fresh quality wherever they go. They will be welcomed with joy into every home. People should acquire magnetic energies from nature and share them with their dear ones. (84X)

You should study the whole of nature. Its every action has an internal significance. And we should rejoice at the goods which nature gives us. (108X)

Nature allots to each person the energy required for his growth. (28X)

In nature there is a great law according to which it accomplishes everything with the least expenditure of energy. Nature likes economy. (19)

Nature works for the good of those who understand it; those noetic people who think, feel and act correctly. (28X)

If it is a question of law and order, we can find it only in living noetic nature. Therefore, having come to the earth, people should study that unchangeable order that exists in nature and live in accordance with it. (26X)

When the energies of the human body operate in harmony with the laws and energies of nature, people feel confident within themselves. (22X)

When a person has led a regular life in the past and does so in the present – a life in unison with the laws of noetic nature – that person enjoys excellent health. (27X)

The felling of the forests and the slaughter of the mammals has brought about great suffering from which humans cannot extricate themselves. They do not suspect that the animals and the plants represent a reservoir of vital energies necessary for human growth and development. When the mammals are slaughtered, their vital energies are dispersed in space. And since people cannot make direct contact with the energies of nature, they are deprived of the energies which they receive through the animals when they are alive. (21X)

Nature has a great abundance at her disposal but it gives out a little at a time. It wants to teach people to be contented with the little which is given them and to fulfil the work assigned to them with that small amount. Learn thus to make noetic use of the small blessings which are given to you during the day. Do not worry: you have eternity in front of you. The blessings of God will not cease; they will flow into your life forever. (3)

Living nature is in no hurry. Before it lies eternity. It has as much time as it wants. It is economical with its energies. People who are in too much of a hurry soon expend their capital of energy and pass over at an early stage. (54)

So long as human beings develop, so will the earth. When they pass into a higher phase of development, the earth will also evolve. The forms of the earth will become more beautiful and perfect. The process of development which the earth is passing through today is slow and even. In the past the development of the earth was rapid and accompanied by great cataclysms. (3)

Crystals were the first form to exist on earth, then plants; later came small animals, then the larger ones followed. Finally, humans appeared. The crystals descended from the world of wisdom. The plants descended from the world of angels. After them came the sons of archangels – the animals; finally came human beings – the image and likeness of God. The conditions for their development, however, were not good, which is why contemporary humans were created – another phase. The human being in the image and likeness of God will come now. And the kind of human beings who are consciously returning to God will take charge of human evolution. These souls are on their way and we will go to meet them. All religions will undergo a transformation of consciousness. You are now approaching the world of the sons of God. (77X)

The path of the seed is from the earth to the branches of the tree. That is what people call evolution. (26X)

People live and develop according to the law of evolution. They should begin with the smallest ideas and units, those which are closest at hand, and then gradually move on to the greater units and more distant objects. Only by applying this law can we expect to achieve anything. (56X)

The roots of your life have to be in the heart, while the branches are in your mind. You should send all the sap up to the branches, towards God. That is evolution: to form your blossoms so that future fruit may ripen. (50)

If you want to evolve and unfold, do not stop at the present state of your life. Take a firm stand and say: 'Evil is necessary to evolution. We are going to live according to the demands of universal love.' (75X)

THE SUN

Light is a sign of love. When the sun shines on us that shows that God is sending us light. Physical light is a sign of God's love. (115X)

The budget of every person, society, nation and indeed of the whole of humanity is determined by the sun. The sun is currently sending more physical energy to the earth, that is to say, people are currently able to accept more physical than spiritual energy from the sun. In the future, people will also be able to receive the spiritual energy of the sun. (28X)

When we say that people should lead pure, sacred and noetic lives, we have in mind that they should tap the appropriate energies of the sun. The more inspired the person, the greater his capacity to make contact with the spiritual energies of the sun. (28X)

The energies of the sun are positive and act favourably on people. The earth energies are negative and act unfavourably on people. The former energies help humanity to rise and the latter to descend. Try to tune into the energies that come from above. (28X)

The sun is the bearer of new ideas, new discoveries, new philosophies, a new religion and a new science. The sun is going to sweep aside everything old; it will consume the old and turn it into dust. The sun will bring to earth a pure and sublime life. For whom will this be so? For the souls that are ready. The soul that is ready is like a bud waiting for the sun to shine. When it does, the bud will open into blossom. (28)

It is good to sunbathe early in the morning – until noon at the latest. If you do this, your mind should be concentrated and positive; you should accept only the positive rays of the sun. You should be careful not to fall asleep or else you will lose everything you have gained. (95X)

I regard the energy of the sun as a living energy. Everything grows, blossoms and ripens in it. That living energy comes only early in the morning when the sun rises. (64X)

The energies that come from the sun contain a store of vital and healing powers. If people wish to make a noetic use of the sun's energies, they should stand with their back to the rays of the sun for half an hour before it rises and direct their thoughts towards it. (76X)

If you go out to meet the sun early in the morning, be there on time before it rises above the horizon. Meet the first ray of the rising sun. It is the most important one; it is the son of truth. It contains the energy and might of the sun. If you do not receive the first ray, you have missed the sunrise. Receive the first ray and calmly return home. The first ray of the sun brings the wealth of all the rays. The first ray is the first fruit of the rising sun, the first fruit of the great tree of life. (13X)

The most luminous thought, the most sublime feeling and the most beautiful action have the first ray of the sun within themselves, the first ray which penetrates the human soul. (13X)

Every morning the sun rises and beings from the invisible world ask you, 'Did you read the page of the book fixed for today?' The sun is a book, and God writes something new in it every day. (21X)

So, in order to renovate yourselves, rise early in the morning and receive the first ray of the sun. It is accompanied by radiant and sublime thoughts. (28X)

One little plant was praying to God: 'God, please visit me with Thy heavenly dew and light, so that my little heart may rejoice at Thy blessing. Lord, I am going to put on my best clothes to meet Thy light. I shall greet everyone who passes my way. I shall greet them in Thy name.' (32X)

THE MOUNTAIN

It is a great boon for people to be in grand and magnificent mountains, surrounded by peaks and valleys. The mountains are reservoirs of energies which help people to transform their mental states. (95X)

From ancient times up to the present day, everyone who has worked and is working in the spiritual field has visited the high mountain peaks. People who understand the laws of the spiritual world have always made noetic use of the high peaks. (26X)

People who would like to improve the state of their lungs should climb high mountains. When the breathing is simultaneously improved, people's spiritual capacity expands accordingly. (26X)

The useful thing about climbing up and down mountain peaks is that a similar ascent and descent takes place in human consciousness. (45X)

Having come to the mountains, we get up early to pray and give thanks to God for all the good gifts which surround us. (45X)

Now that you have come to the mountains, you should live well so as not to stain nature as part of the whole creation. You ought all to have pure thoughts and feelings, lest you violate the harmony of nature. The slightest violation has dire consequences. (26X)

When you climb the mountain, do not be in a hurry to go down again. Choose the most beautiful place and sit down to rest. Survey all the scenery around you and record the beautiful picture within your soul. When you go down into the valley, retain the living picture in your memory; remember the living peak you have climbed. The high mountain peaks and the pure mountain springs are alive and they leave an imprint of eternal and indelible images within human consciousness. (13X)

When you walk in the mountains, walk slowly and calmly without hurrying. Stop to rest for about half a minute every hundred metres or so. During this time of rest, you are acquiring energy. The higher you climb, the slower you should walk. In this way you will adjust to the forces of nature and will make correct use of them. Otherwise, they will oppose you, in which case you will expend your energy in vain. Every particle of the mountain is connected with the Primary Principle which is working within nature. So when you climb the mountain peaks, reflect on the service they are performing in nature in order to make contact with the noetic element in every mountain, summit and lake. Wherever you go, work consciously, studying and applying what you know. (3)

The mountain spring is alive. A sublime spirit has sat near it from time immemorial, working and fulfilling its predestined role. If you come to a mountain spring, you should stop reverently in front of it; you should take your hat off, wash your face and drink some of its water. Then you will say, 'Lord, help me clean my heart and enlighten my mind like the water of this spring.' When you go to a mountain spring, drink its water, wash your face and give thanks. (14X)

Be contented and joyful so as to use the benefits offered by the mountain with its fresh air, pure water and the magnificent beauty of its scenery. (26X)

If you cannot climb up and down Moussala [the highest peak in the Rila mountains], you cannot be disciples. Climbing Moussala is a difficult examination, especially in the evening or on a snowy winter's night. First, you will make the attempt during the day; then on a moonlit evening, and the third time on a dark night when the peak is capped with snow. The task is an arduous one, but you should attempt it. If you are not inwardly prepared, you will do only the first assignment by going to Moussala during the day. That is not easy either. It is difficult for a person to pass through the Rila desert all alone – the desert where no bird flies. The person walks along, hearing his own footsteps from time to time, hearing the wind blow through the leaves. His hair may stand on end out of fear, especially in late evening. The person who performs this experiment will acquire something fine in his character. When the person crosses the Rila desert, he will grow more serious the further he goes. But he will later become joyful. His heart will expand and he will experience an overwhelming gratitude to God for having been able to pass through the valley of silence. People grow when they find themselves between opposing sets of conditions. In this way they get to know themselves and become acquainted with the great and sublime in the world. (95X)

It is not sufficient to fight for the first place – you should deserve it. The person aspiring for the first place should start for Moussala in the evening, passing through the Rila desert and coming back down. This is a task only for heroes. Those who are not heroes may take the same route, but in twos or threes. Disciples in the past were given similar tests. Adepts and saints have all walked along this path. They have climbed all the high peaks. The peaks a person climbs in the course of his life are a measure of his achievements. (95X)

9

The New Epoch

The words of the Master Beinsa Douno on the new epoch are words of prophecy and inspiration. He came to sow seeds which might take generations to germinate, the seeds of a new culture of love, cooperation, understanding and mutual aid when human beings will become conscious of their context and role within a larger organic whole. This culture will become realized as it slowly but surely seeps through into human consciousness; we shall become increasingly aware of our interconnectedness and interdependence. As yet, the process is for the most part unconscious and unfamiliar: the new grows up through the disintegration of the old.

The force of renewal is the force of love: not love as an aspiration in the heart or even as a feeling in the soul; but love as a force in the mind and a principle in the spirit; love as a means of harmonizing the contradictions of human existence. The renewal is not immediately apparent since it is a process which works outwards from the depths within. The first changes take place in our minds and hearts, leading to changes of action inspired by the high ideal of devotion to the Kingdom of God.

Within our own limited spheres we all have a responsible contribution to make towards cultural renewal through working on our minds, hearts and wills as we refine our nature and develop latent talents and virtues in the light of the great principles of love, wisdom and truth. If we persist in our struggles and aspirations, the seeds within us will surely bear fruit, bringing joy and peace to ourselves and others in the process:

'*People often ask about the goal of life. The answer is simple: we live in order to form just, pure and balanced thoughts, to refine our feelings, to purify our heart, to strengthen our will and learn how best to use it.*'

The following prayer, said three times, is the prayer of the disciple, composed by the Master Beinsa Douno:

> *May we have:*
> *A heart as pure as a crystal,*
> *A mind as radiant as the sun,*
> *A soul as vast as the universe,*
> *A spirit as powerful as God and one with God.*

Another formula:

> *May I love as God loves,*
> *May I sing as God sings,*
> *May the Kingdom of God come on earth,*
> *May I be a bearer of His light.*

Finally, the blessing of the Master:

> *May love be with you – it will bring you peace, joy and gratitude.*

> *May the love of the Holy Spirit shine within you.*
> *Be contented in the spirit.*
> *The sun of life is eternal radiance.*

> *May My peace be with you all who dwell in divine purity.*

> *May My light and love be always within you, disciples of life!*

•   •   •

The Lord is coming with His fire to clear up the earth, to remove old clothing, to give new bodies, to bring love into hearts, to raise minds and put away all malice and hatred. This is the signature and the divine creed of the new epoch. (31X)

We are entering a period of liquidation. Meanwhile, people must change themselves. They should remove the old and useless, retaining only the sound and useful elements in life. (56X)

A new law and order are coming into the world. That new order requires new people – heroes. That order excludes disease, crime and violence. (32X)

It is only love that has the power to set the world to rights. (26)

In order to improve conditions on earth, people must love. Love satisfies every need. It contains all good conditions and possibilities. It is a mighty transformer of all forces. A special light emanates from the person who has been visited by love. (14)

The earth is moving towards the harbour of love. It is entering a new sphere where different forces are in operation. When this century comes to an end, the people will raise white banners. They will arrive at the frontiers of the Kingdom of God and they will say: 'Long live love! Long live wisdom! Long live truth!' People will help one another and will begin to live in peace and love, in brotherhood and freedom. (25X)

The only God that persists is love. Love is now coming into the world. A great power is coming into the world and you are going to change unconsciously. That love will come and remove everything from you – you are going to change. One day you will awaken and realize that your mind has changed. (5X)

All people are aspiring towards the new, towards the new life. The new life, however, requires new conceptions. In the new life the idea of father, mother, brother, sister, teacher and student will be entirely different. The person who has not been penetrated by the new ideas cannot enter the new life. No kind of reconstruction can be brought about without new ideas. (3)

All conscious people in the world today are in a state of expectation. They are expecting something good of life. That is the new which is on its way. Everyone senses it. It already permeates the air and penetrates the whole of life. (14)

I ask you: How can humanity emerge from its present condition? Today people must come up with new thinking to resolve all the issues. The resolution of these issues represents a problem for the whole of humanity. All must participate in this great problem which is of equal concern to all people. Contemporary nations are conscious of this and are working towards a solution. (56)

The future world is a world of love and understanding between people; it will be a world of brotherhood and freedom. (32X)

Our task is to bring about the Kingdom of God on earth. We want to be conductors of the divine law. May that law rule all minds and hearts; may all men and women become sons and daughters of the divine kingdom and may they begin to live on the earth accordingly! (31X)

Many people first expect life to improve before they themselves become good. This would mean that the idea of the good should first be applied in life and then in human beings. This is not possible. People expect the Kingdom of God to come from outside before it enters into them. They expect it to come from outside in some spiritual way and that they will immediately acquire the right to citizenship in this kingdom. But this can never happen. The Kingdom of God is within people and not outside them. (3)

All future benefits and goods in life will spring from an understanding of the external conditions and inner possibilities. (14)

Many think that they must first put their affairs in order and then serve God. This is not right: serve God every minute, every hour and in all circumstances. If you want to put your life in order before serving God, you will lose your present favourable conditions. I am suggesting this thought to you so that you always remember that you are cords as fine as a spider's web. If these cords are not united, they will not withstand external storms and winds. Thousands of cords combined into a whole make something solid and durable. If you each live for yourself without becoming united, your strength will be equivalent to the web and you will accomplish only as much as the spider. If, however, you become united you will carry out the necessary work, for God's work is being done by many people and not simply by a single person. Many people are predestined to accomplish God's work. (3)

Do not wait for the world to be arranged before you correct yourself! That is what the new creed demands! (85X)

Everyone should desire the coming of the Kingdom of God on earth. Everyone should desire that the will of God be done on earth. Everyone should stand on the side of wisdom, desiring the coming of light and knowledge. Everyone should stand on the side of truth and wish to acquire freedom. This is the only way in which you will become conductors of the divine and overcome all hardships. All of you are entrusted to carry out your missions as you should. God has given you excellent bodies, luminous minds, noble hearts, strong wills, and you have to develop these qualities. God has also given you a powerful spirit and a great soul; in return, you should willingly and lovingly accomplish His will.
The person who realizes this has to say: 'We are all going to work as awakened souls for the coming of the Kingdom of God on earth.' (40)

When people begin to love one another as brothers and sisters and are prepared to share their goods without violence, at that moment we can say that God has come to earth. There is no other way for God to come among the people. This is the only way by which people may expect the coming of the Kingdom of God on earth. (38)

When Christ comes to earth, all people will be resurrected. I mean that when all people come to love each other, then there will be no hunger, no poverty, no illness, no misunderstanding. Then houses and purses will be opened for each other. Then all will come to know God, and God will reveal Himself. Then love will be the law for all. (4)

The love of God unites all people. This is a great truth which is tested every day. (3)

The new creed is coming to the world to bring brotherhood and sisterhood among the peoples of the earth, to make them work for one another. A day will come when this idea will be realized, the day of the new epoch will come, the era of the rising sun. (47)

What does the new creed represent? It liberates the human mind, heart and consciousness. No burden remains. If you are poor, it will remove the burden of poverty; if you are hungry, it will release you from hunger; if you are fearful, it will liberate you from fear; if you are vain, it will free you from vanity; if you are proud, it will free you from pride; if you are greedy, it will free you from greed. As long as you retain these negative states in your consciousness, you will not be able to achieve anything. (85X)

Love brings life, wisdom brings light and knowledge, while truth brings freedom. Love is fundamental to life, while light, knowledge and freedom are conditions for the manifestation of love. (89X)

The new is different from the old in that it creates a link between love and wisdom. (27X)

The mind will commit itself to helping with good deeds; the heart will come to help love, the will to help truth, while your soul will be entirely committed to helping God's wisdom. (65X)

When I speak to you about new conceptions of life, I do not mean that you should do away with the old straight away, that is, destroy it. The old will remain as a fertilizer in which you will plant the new ideas. (28X)

Leave the old creed to function in the roots, while the new one works in the branches. Nowadays, people need a new conception of life expressed in new forms created by new thoughts and new feelings. (87X)

First of all you have to love the Lord with your whole heart, soul, mind and power; then you should love your neighbour as yourself; and third, you should love your enemies. (31X)

It is most important for you to help each other. Therein lies the new creed: mutual aid. (25X)

The divine creed is a creed of living experience. Talking alone is not enough – application is the main requirement. (39X)

Brothers and sisters, love one another and help one another – that is what the divine creed asks of people in the world. (64X)

Being brothers and sisters means first of all purity. Purity in what respect? Purity in thoughts, desires and actions. There should be an expansion of the mind and heart. (86X)

You will know your brother when you are wounded, when you are unhappy: he will embrace you, give you a kiss and take you to his home. Your sister will do the same thing. (86X)

We people of the new teaching must be distinguished not by means of our piety, knowledge, power or goodness, but through our love. This is the natural way. (6)

Everything on earth which is done with disinterestedness, love, wisdom and light brings concord. Wherever there is concord everything can be achieved. (97X)

The only necessary attainment for contemporary people is brotherhood – a brotherhood of noetic people. By the word 'brotherhood' I mean the gift of the rights and conditions to develop what God has implanted within and not to impede progress. The progress of a single person is the progress of the whole of humanity. (97X)

Link yourselves with all good people who work with love for the divine cause – no matter what their creed and nationality. Only in this way will people understand why they have come to earth. (39X)

We are members of this world and must fulfil the will of God whatever it may be. This is the great law of eternal life. This is the great law for all disciples who desire the realization of the good as it is written in the divine book which has not yet been printed on earth. (6)

From what should people free themselves? From all the existing aberrations in the world. They will then emerge into a full light and will be in contact with all good people who have understood the law of God. (97X)

You all need the new knowledge, the knowledge of the spirit, the knowledge of love. (56X)

As soon as you find love, you will know the inner meaning of life. In this way you will love everything in the world: animals, plants and even every stone. Love everything but do not strive to possess anything. Wherever you see the great love – in the grain of wheat, in the ray of the sun or in a human being – keep it pure and sacred. If you can maintain all this in a spirit of purity, you have entered the path on which everything can be revealed to you. In this way you will think more of others than of yourself. Then you will no longer ask how the world will be set right. You will know that the world in which you live is all right. (3)

We do not want to make people believe in God, but we want everyone to use divine light and warmth, divine knowledge and freedom. (27X)

Before the rising of the sun in human consciousness, one lives between the two forces of pressure and tension, unable to balance and harmonize them. As soon as the sun – the noetic principle – rises within, the person easily copes with these forces. After harmonizing these opposing forces within themselves, people begin to manifest creative powers and devote themselves to conscious noetic work. In order to attain this state, one must study and acquire divine knowledge. The noetic person works continuously in the service of the whole and its parts. These laws apply to the individual, the family, society, the nation and humanity as a whole. They operate everywhere in life and nature. (14)

People expect the sun to rise so that they can enjoy its light and heat. According to me it does not matter if it is only the external sun which has risen. If the outer sun has risen but the inner human sun has not done so, nothing is gained. It is a significant moment when the rising of the outer sun corresponds to the rising of the inner sun. This is a real sunrise. The outer sun is valuable for all living beings, while the inner sun is significant for human beings. There is no greater joy than seeing both within and without. Great is the joy of the human being and of the whole of heaven when all people on earth understand and know their Creator. Then the Kingdom of God has come on earth. (5)

People today want to be loved. The desire is right, but it is not sufficient to be loved by a single person. The human being represents a microscopic tube through which only a single sunbeam can pass. This sunbeam will contribute something to life, but the most powerful thing in the world is the whole sun. The light of the whole sun must enter into people and illuminate even the remotest corner of their house. One sunbeam is the love of a single person. This is not sufficient. Love which cannot transform people, making them healthy, good and wise, is not worthy of the name. Love is that power which transforms human beings and makes them prepared for every kind of sacrifice for the sake of the secret name upon which life rests. The real sacrifice is the sacrifice for the Creator of the universe, for the Sacred One, not a sacrifice simply for people. Where will you find the Sacred One? He is hidden in the soul of all living beings. A great sacrifice is required of all people, as it was of Christ. Of what does that sacrifice consist? When they are nailed to the cross in the name of God and say: 'Father forgive them.' (3)

THE FUTURE CULTURE

Culture is the outcome of the efforts of higher beings. They work on the minds of people, bringing them light. In the meantime, they instil elevated impulses, noble desires and feelings. When people realize this, they will understand that culture is nothing other than the conscious work by noetic beings on the whole of humanity. Music, poetry, art and science, which confer significance on our lives, descend from the higher world as ideas and are realized on earth. Wise beings will come to earth to arrange life in this way – that is the future culture. (36–31)

As long as a person does good deeds they will always have conditions to unfold properly and progress gradually into the ideas of the new culture and the new life. (18–71)

Desires and thoughts create the present world. If we begin to talk about love, love will come. If we begin to talk about freedom, freedom will come. (109X–43)

In its development, the present culture is moving like an ascending spiral. After this culture, that of the fifth race, will come the culture of the sixth. It is a culture of the feelings and the heart. It is one of the sublime cultures. In that culture both heart and mind will be able to unfold properly. (28–202)

The new culture is on the way! Human thoughts and feelings have to be regulated and then those called the 'geniuses of humanity' will come and undertake the upliftment of humanity. That is great work! The uplifting of humanity is not the work of one person alone. (105X–410)

The spiritual element is coming into the world. That is why future writers, poets, playwrights and musicians have to bring that spiritual element into their works. (14–88)

Everything that is coming is the divine love which is going to bring law and order among the people. Law and order will come and future people will know one another and begin to live fraternally. At the time when these ideas of fraternity are realized, rulers will be wise. Teachers, professors and mothers will be learned and wise. They will be brothers and sisters to one another and the earth will be a place of blessing. (105X–183)

Good people from all parts of the earth will lend each other a hand and will unite in the name of divine love, wisdom and truth. And they will bring in the new culture with all its benefits and achievements. Great is the future of the earth. God is manifesting in the world. (14X)

The sublime beings from the invisible world, who have completed their evolution, are looking for co-workers in the new culture: people with pure hearts and radiant minds. Do you imagine that God Himself and the angels will come to the earth in order to settle human affairs? They will manifest themselves through those who are ready and willing on the earth. (14–114)

All great musicians, poets, artists and scientists are working for the salvation of humanity. The invisible world will uplift people through them. (14–117)

In the present epoch of extreme individualization, separate individuals and nations are too far apart from each other. Each lives for itself, pursuing personal ends and interests. Today it is not just separate individuals but whole societies and nations which find themselves subjected to great pressure and tension, up against difficult situations and possibilities which they are unable to resolve and balance. All this shows the great need for the influx of a new stream of life forces, not only in the individual but also in social and international life. And this stream is already beginning to flow into life. It induces the right relations of the part to the whole. Would the cells and organs of the human organism function normally if they were to become isolated and individualized, breaking away from the organism? In the same way, separate individuals, societies and nations must become conscious of themselves as a great whole, as parts of the human organism; in this way they will bring about a fundamental change in the forms of life. Every part must realize that its success and welfare depends upon the success and welfare of the whole organism. This is the new understanding of life. This is the sun which is presently rising in human consciousness. This is the new life stream which has begun to operate and whose influence is becoming more powerful by the day in all spheres of life. It will flood all societies and nations, laying the foundation of a beautiful, noetic and harmonious life on earth.

Humanity is currently on the cusp between two cultures, two epochs. A new epoch is approaching in which all erroneous ideas, by which people have hitherto lived, will be transformed. The new earth and the new heaven will be shaped out of the present form of life. People will regard each other as brothers and sisters, and will be ready to sacrifice themselves for each other.

The present world is destined to undergo a great transformation. Paradise is a place where all beings love each other and live for each other. In the new conception of life, people see that what is good for themselves is good for everybody. The new consciousness and new understanding will effect a fundamental transformation in the whole order of life. Then work will be regarded in a new light. Love will be the incentive for the new forms of work.

The coming epoch will be a bright future. At the present time, however, humanity is passing through a dark zone. The new epoch can be called an epoch of resurrection. Resurrection in this sense is nothing other than divine love awakening human consciousness and bringing it to life.

In the future, all nations will enjoy brotherly relations and will evolve as a shining race of love. Then the sacred flame of the true life will be manifest in all its beauty. Life will not be manifest in its shadows, but in its essence.

The present sufferings are the birth pangs of the new human being. The new is approaching the earth with silent steps like the dawn which proclaims the coming of the new day in the world. (14)

References

Where a single reference number is given it refers to the title listed below. Where two numbers are given the first refers to the title and the second to the page number within the volume.

All titles are by Peter K. Deunov – Beinsa Douno.
1. *Songs of the Master*, Sofia, 1938.
2. *Our Place*, Sofia, 1931.
3. *The Royal Path of the Soul*, Sofia, 1935.
4. *The Garment of Life* (1932–3), Sofia, 1950.
5. *The Sower* (1932–3), Sofia, 1950.
6. *The Path of the Disciple* (1927), Sofia.
7. *The Five Brothers* (1923), Sofia, 1949.
8. *Power and Life*, vol. III (1921–2), Sofia, 1922.
9. *Touching Points of Nature* (1922–3), Sofia, 1935.
10. *Liquidation of this Age* (1937–8), Sofia, 1948.
11. *Rules of the Occult School* (1923), Sofia.
12. *Order and Instructions for Every Day* (1925), Ternovo.
13. *Good Habits* (1923), Sofia, 1936.
14. *The New Day* (1940), Sofia.
15. *Conditions for Growth* (1930), Sofia, 1939.
16. *The Holy Place* (1927), Sofia, 1939.
17. *Contradictions in Life* (1922), Sofia, 1934.
18. *The Two Ways* (1922), Sofia, 1934.
19. *Lectures IV, V, VI of the Young People's Occult Class* (1925), Sofia, 1929.
20. *Sacred Words of the Master* (1935), Sofia.
21. *Congress Lectures* (5–8, viii, 1925), Sofia.
22. *The Noetic Life* (1923), Sofia, 1926.
23. *Positive and Negative Forces in Nature* (1922), Sofia.
24. *Occult Medicine* (1922), Sofia.
25. *The Direction of Growth* (1926–7), Sofia, 1938.
26. *The Three Lives* (1922), Sofia.

27. *The Influence of Light and Darkness* (1925–6), Sofia, 1927.
28. *The New Thought* (1932), Sofia, 1947.
29. *Absolute Purity* (1929), Sofia.
30. *The Two Methods of Nature* (1923–4), Sofia, 1924.
31. *The Divine Thought* (1927–8), Sofia, 1942.
32. *The Deeds of God* (1930), Sofia, 1942.
33. *Entering* (1927), Sofia, 1930.
34. *The Living Lord* (1922), Sofia, 1948.
35. *The Divine Conditions* (1928–9), Sofia, 1942.
36. *The High Ideal* (1923), Sofia.
37. *The Law of Unity and Community* (1928), Sofia.
38. *Spirit and Flesh* (1927), Sofia.
39. *The Testament of Love*, vol. III (1944), Sofia.
40. *The Testament of the Colour Rays* (1912), Sofia, 1940.
41. *Definite Movements* (1929), Sofia, 1939.
42. *Two Sacred Positions* (1925), Ternovo.
43. *Lectures of the Young People's Class* (1925), Sofia, 1929.
44. *The Correct Distribution of Energy* (1923), Sofia.
45. *The Living Word* (1926–7), Sofia, 1937.
46. *The Future Creed of Humanity* (1933), Sofia, 1934.
47. *The Language of Love* (1935), Sofia.
48. *Laws of Good* (1930), Sofia, 1940.
49. *The Beginning of Wisdom*, Sofia, 1947.
50. *The Three Directions* (1933), Sofia, 1948.
51. *The Motive Powers of Life* (1938), Sofia.
52. *The Meaning of Contradictions* (1923), Sofia.
53. *The Unsolved* (1926–7), Sofia, 1933.
54. *He Knows* (1925), Sofia, 1926.
55. *The Testament of Love*, vol. I (1944), Sofia.
56. *The New Eve* (1931), Sofia.
57. *Converses and Instructions of the Master* (1921), Ternovo.
1X. *Absolute Truth* (1930–2), Sofia.
2X. *Absolute Justice* (1924), Sofia.
3X. See 29.
4X. *Converses, Explanations and Instructions* (1919), Ternovo.
5X. See 57.
6X. *Blessed among Women* (1930), Sofia.
7X. See 31.
8X. *The Voice of God* (1930), Sofia.
9X. See 46.
10X. *The Great Noetic Principle* (1932–3), Sofia.

11X. *Eternal Rejuvenation* (1945), Sofia.
12X. *The Eternal Good* (1943), Sofia.
13X. See 36.
14X. See 33.
15X. *Converses and Instructions on the Congress* (1920), Ternovo.
16–18X. *Rules of the Occult School* (1923), Sofia.
19X. See 27.
20X. *All That is Written* (1917), Sofia.
21X. *Possibilities for Happiness* (1942), Sofia.
22X. *Eternal Expression* (unpublished).
23X. *The Great Brother* (1923), Sofia.
24X. See 26.
25X. See 18.
26X. See 51.
27X. See 32.
28X. See 13.
29X. See 9.
30X. *The End of the Century* (1926), Sofia.
31X. See 38.
32X. *The Language of Love* (1939), Sofia.
33X. *The Natural Order of Things* (1929), Sofia.
34X. *The Living Word* (1937), Sofia.
35X. *Life for the Whole* (1939), Sofia.
36X. *Life and Relations* (1931), Sofia.
37X. *The Testament of Love*, vol. II (1944), Sofia.
38X. See 39.
39X. See 37.
40X. *Power and Life*, vol. V (1922), Sofia.
41X. See 12.
42X. *The Cosmic and the Ordinary* (1919), Sofia.
43X. *The Beauty of the Soul* (1938), Sofia.
44X. See 10.
45X. *Love towards God* (1931), Sofia.
46X. *Methods for Self-Education* (1930–31), Sofia.
47X. *The Kingdom of God has Come* (1925), Sofia.
48X. *Everyday Thoughts* (unpublished).
49X. *Inner and Outer Bonds* (1926), Sofia.
50–52X. See 16–18X.
53X. See 12.
54X. See 49.
55X. See 2.
56X. See 59.
57X. See 56.

58X. See 28.
59X. *The New Life* (1922), Sofia.
60X. *The New Conceptions of the Disciple* (1927), Sofia.
61X. *The New Humanity* (1947), Sofia.
63X. See 14.
64X. *The New Man* (1947), Sofia.
65X. See 57.
66-7X. See 16-18X.
68X. See 36.
69X. *Occult Music* (1922), Sofia.
70X. *Points of Support in Life* (1942), Sofia.
71X. See 41.
72X. *Father Loves Me* (1936), Sofia.
73X. *The Simple Truths* (1933), Sofia.
74X. See 16X.
75X. See 23.
76X. See 25.
77X. See 16X.
78X. *You Have Judged Rightly* (1930), Sofia.
79-80X. See 16X.
81X. See 17.
82X. *The Way of the Disciple* (1927), Sofia.
83X. See 22.
84X. *The Holy Place* (1924), Sofia.
85X. See 5.
86X. See 8.
87X. *Factors in Nature* (1947), Sofia.
88X. See 8.
89X. *The Old is Gone* (1927), Sofia.
90X. *Stages of Consciousness* (1939), Sofia.
91X. *Awakening* (1931-2) Sofia.
92X. *Proportionality in Nature* (1949), Sofia.
93X. *He Creates* (1936-7), Sofia.
94X. See 16X.
95X. See 26.
96X. See 50.
97X. See 15.
98X. *Study and Work* (1934), Sofia.
99X. *Forces in Nature* (1938), Sofia.
100X. *The Valuable Word* (1941), Sofia.
101X. *The Valuable from the Book of Great Life* (1932), Sofia
102X. *Pure and Luminous* (1926), Sofia.
103X. See 43.
104X. *The Good Weapon* (1934), Sofia.

105X. *Everyday Thoughts* (1983), unpublished.
106X. *Everyday Thoughts* (1985), unpublished.
107X. See 16X.
108X. *Power and Life* (1921), Sofia.
109X. See 30.
110X. *Everyday Thoughts* (1988), unpublished.
111X. See 34.
112X. *He was Teaching Them* (1949), Sofia.
113X. See 35.
114X. *Conditions for the Noetic Man* (1926), Sofia.
115X. See 30.
116X. See 26.
117X. See 30.
118X. *Possible Attainments* (1927), Sofia.
119X. *Everyday Thoughts* (1984), unpublished.
120X. *Everyday Thoughts* (1986), unpublished
121X. *The Great Conditions of Life* (1944), Sofia.
122X. See 16X.

Printed in the United Kingdom
by Lightning Source UK Ltd.
1415